Kisses from the U.S. Government

Patrick Kelly

We at Trafford believe that it is the responsibility of us all, as both individuals and corporations, to make choices that are environmentally and socially sound. You, in turn, are supporting this responsible conduct each time you purchase a Trafford book, or make use of our publishing services. To find out how you are helping, please visit www.trafford.com/responsiblepublishing.html

Our mission is to efficiently provide the world's finest, most comprehensive book publishing service, enabling every author to experience success. To find out how to publish your book, your way, and have it available worldwide, visit us online at www.trafford.com/10510

Trafford rev. 7/13/2009

 www.trafford.com

North America & international
toll-free: 1 888 232 4444 (USA & Canada)
phone: 250 383 6864 ♦ fax: 250 383 6804 ♦ email: info@trafford.com

The United Kingdom & Europe
phone: +44 (0)1865 487 395 ♦ local rate: 0845 230 9601
facsimile: +44 (0)1865 481 507 ♦ email: info.uk@trafford.com

Table of Contents

Overview

"Boom and Bust; Boom and Bust; Boom and Bust." This is the mantra of the powers that control world finances and economies, including the United States. This is the mantra that has led America into 19 recessions and the Great Depression of 1929, in the relatively short period of time since 1916.

The current recession started in October of 2007, although it was not officially acknowledged as a recession until the end of 2008, after twelve months of clear recessionary statistics and reality, despite the continued banter that it was only an economic slowdown and everything was working just fine.

Boom and Bust is the mantra of the world financial powers, controlling economies throughout the world, just as they are the controlling forces of the Federal Reserve Bank, a privately owned bank and not a government agency. The Fed is often referred to as a quasi-public/government agency, which is a government entity with private components.

The Federal Reserve Bank controls the economy. They can manipulate, deflate, inflate and move the markets as they see fit by releasing more money into the economy, backed by absolutely nothing but an accountant's ledger adjustment, to make things happen. As manipulations occur, the American people end up with a higher interest liability to the Federal Reserve for the money it has printed.

What happened to the basic principle that you need to HAVE money to LEND money? The Federal Reserve Bank has the authority and the ability to create money out of thin air and then charge interest for lending that money. If the Federal Reserve were a government agency, they would be able to erase the federal deficit and if the Federal Reserve Bank were a private entity then it would surely have been audited at some point. But the Federal Reserve Bank has never been audited. It has no assets. It has credit for interest on debts that it has created and the American people are forced to pay the interest on these debts to the private owners of the Federal Reserve.

When the Federal Reserve Act of 1913 passed Congress, a majority of the voting went directly along party lines, in much the same manner as the stimulus packages and bailouts are being voted again in the current economic crisis. In 1913, most Democrats were in support of the Federal Reserve Act and most Republicans were against it. History repeats itself with "de ja vu" all over again.

The stock market crash of 1929 was a well- orchestrated attack on the American financial system and the American people. The stock market was growing, people had jobs, they had more money in their pockets and life was good for them. They had money to invest and the stock market appeared to be the way to grow their money as compared to placing it in a savings account with a low fixed interest rate.

With this came an opportunity to steal from the American people. No need for guns or violence, they would steal the money the same way as they created it; by producing a fictitious financial system based on an arbitrary number for a stock. As the public started to invest in the stock market, there was more and more money to buy the stocks they wanted, which drove the prices up. This created paper wealth for most and true wealth for those that would ultimately sell their stock for gains.

This is not a system that is going to take the money from everyone at the same time, because if that happened, it would clearly be seen as the theft and deception that it is. This is a calculated scheme to remove the assets from a percentage of people and redistribute it to the controlling forces of the organized powers that control the world's finances.

Liken it to the gambling casinos. The odds are all in the favor of the house at the casinos. They are not looking to take all of the money at one time. They have their hands in the right places to put the odds in their favor. Even those who do win big at the casinos have ample opportunities to give it back in the form of high-priced stores that are located outside the casino. Everything is calculated and nothing is left to chance.

But it's the actual gambling that makes the casino the money. Gamblers may sit at the table for two minutes or they could be there for hours and hours. Regardless of the amount of time, the results are the same. The casino normally has all of the money and the gambler leaves feeling as if they have lost the money on a fair and equal playing field. Maybe next time they will be the lucky one and walk away with the casino's money.

The stock market does relatively the same thing as a black-jack table. Americans with money want into the stock market so they can be part of the growth. Many people who have money in the stock market are also carrying debt as they gamble in the stocks. Instead of paying off their debts with the money, they have borrowed the money to gamble with. As more people do this, they continue to buy stocks. The same stock that was worth five dollars on Monday is now worth $10 on Tuesday, very often with nothing different about the company, it's operations, it's earnings or it's forecasts. The price of the stock has increased because there are more people buying that stock. As it continues to go up, there will be more people to notice and interest will increase.

It's a self-fulfilling prophecy that the stock price will go up as there is more demand for the stock. Why aren't stock prices based on their values to the investor? What dividends do they pay as a return to the investor and what are their price earning ratio and other details that show the return to the investor? There are statistics and details about every stock and most consumers do not know what they mean. They trust their money to the investors and the traders that are paid in two ways; 1) to make trades, regardless of whether they are good or bad and 2) based on a percentage of the account balance, so their interest does lie in making the account balance bigger.

But herein lie some of the fundamental problems with the system. Traders make trades to earn commissions and that forms their compensation. As investors do well, it attracts more money to buy the same supply of stocks, and the prices of the stocks rise. The paper value of the stock and the portfolio also rises. But the actual profit on that stock is only realized when it is sold. Since Americans have been sold on the "Buy and Hold" strategy and "Dollar Cost Averaging" and keeping money in for real gains over the longer periods of time, it's no wonder that many individual investors will never realize those gains as they have lost not only their profits and gains from their investments but also much of the principle funds they invested.

Many stock and retirement accounts are down fifty to sixty percent from their highs. These are amounts that will never be recovered, possibly in the lifetimes of many account owners. They have saved their entire lives, they have put money away as was suggested to them and they lived within their means. Many of them have lost their life savings. And we are not talking about the victims of the Bernie Madoff and other ponzi schemes. These people were attracted to better returns than are either normal or available to the average person and they became victims of lies and deception.

While we are sold on the "Buy and Hold" strategy the "Boom and Bust" game is being played to steal the savings of average Americans. What justified the Dow Jones Industrial Averages to reach near 14,000 for a high? What justifies a 100 point increase to the DOW every day otherwise it is considered a bad day? How can the stock markets be continually going up? Bottom line is it can't, which is why it was around 8,000 at the beginning of 2009.

Stocks being sold caused the stock market to go down. Was it the average person that owned stocks that sold at the top? Of course not! It was the investors that were controlling the markets, either directly or indirectly. Dollar cost averaging as the stocks continue to grow and then pull your money out ahead of the others will ultimately provide the best returns. Being the first one as a stock price starts to rise and the first one out as it hits the peak is obviously the most profitable.

It's easy to see the benefits of that scenario. As for everyone else who started buying the stock later, and who sold it later after it started to decline, many of them will still make a profit. It will depend specifically on when they got in and when they got out. While there will be some that make profits, many will take losses and chalk it up to bad timing. It's not bad timing, it is market manipulation and corruption! It is another example of the market makers moving markets and prices with the purpose of stealing from average Americans.

Losses will range from small to everything. The last people to buy the stock will take the biggest hit. They may panic and sell as it starts to go down to minimize their losses or they may ride the wave all the way down and wait, using the "Buy and Hold" strategy, with the hopes that the stock will again go back up.

In the meantime, the players that moved the market have taken their profits up front. We also need to remember that many people borrow funds for investment purposes, sometimes as a lien against their home and sometimes as another loan type. They borrow additional funds, increase their debt load, don't pay off other debt that could have been eliminated and then they invest in the stock market where they take a loss. Not only have they lost that money, but they continue to have the original debt plus interest, and have placed their homes and possessions and sometimes businesses at risk.

Now, consider the super-sized version of the stock manipulation program. Instead of subtle market movement or individual stocks being used, they extend it to a specific market, such as the "Dot. com Bubble" or the real estate housing bubble. With the dot. com bubble, as the industry grew and stocks soared, there were many paper millionaires waiting for their stock options to vest. This would allow them to take their deferred cash as many had taken lower paying jobs with the understanding that the stock options would be worth as much or more than their traditional compensation. When that bubble burst, much of the money went to the manipulators.

With the housing bubble, it was the Democrats under Bill Clinton that pressured the mortgage lenders and the banks to make home ownership more available to lower income families. While the bubble officially collapsed during George W. Bush's presidency, the seeds were planted and things were put into motion with the Clinton Administration.

Millions of people will lose their homes and their jobs because of the Depression of 2009. They have yet to label this a depression, but give them the time as it took them a year to acknowledge the Recession of 2008. Some homeowners will lose their homes because they never should have gotten a home loan in the first place. One-hundred percent financing for a borrower with a mediocre credit score without verifying income, assets and sometimes even employment was the Alt-A product line. The sub-prime programs which are blamed for the initial crisis, took clients that could clearly not pay their bills and provided them with financing that was ultimately going to be unmanageable as the adjustments to the interest rates occurred.

Some homeowners will lose their jobs as a result of the overall economy. These are owners that may have lived in their homes for years and years. They may have had a good percentage of equity in the property, seen as their retirement account or the funds for their children's college expenses. That equity vanished quickly but left many with remaining equity. Those without equity often walked away from the homes or let them go into foreclosure.

Consumers have learned to live their lives as the government runs the country. They live pay check to pay check and rely on debt to do more. The government's deficit mentality has become a way of life. Consumers are expected to be fiscally responsible when our government and our leaders can't do what they preach. Tax rates continue to rise. As unemployment numbers increase, the only area still hiring is government. As there are less people generating income to pay taxes and more people collecting unemployment they need more government employees to handle the paperwork.

The government has provided the Federal Reserve and the parties that control it, free reign to steal from the citizens through this "Boom and Bust" society. Not once, not twice, but over and over again we are duped and taken advantage of through recession after recession. Every time the economy hits a point that will allow significant profitability for the governing forces, the average person is subject to loss.

Also like in the casinos, not everyone loses at the same time. The dot.com bubble hit a specific area and industry but those not associated with that industry saw what was happening and could not comprehend the impact it was having on their lives. For the housing bubble, it has affected many more because of the overall impact on the complete economic picture. As housing goes, so goes the economy. Banks, mortgage companies, Realtors, attorneys, title companies, insurance companies and more are being directly affected by the situation. This is compounded by consumers not having equity to access from their homes any more, which affects many other industries. The auto industry was hit hard as cash flow dried up and fear about unemployment rose. Poor sales for the major three US car manufacturers nearly bankrupted them and they ended up needing money from the government to stay in business.

Officials of the United States government have been working to help "Main Street", meaning the small businesses and consumers, but they have clearly shown their true support for "Wall Street" and big business. This is no surprise, given the amount of lobbying money spent on the politicians. The amount of money disclosed is just the tip of the iceberg. Can you imagine the real amount of money that changes hands? Politicians, regardless of their best intentions when they run for office, always remember who got them elected and normally that carries an agenda which may or may not be good for Americans.

The government has provided money to Wall Street banks and firms, where compensation and bonuses were at ridiculous levels. Retention bonuses for employees designed to keep them from leaving the firm to go to a competitor. There are very few competitors remaining. Most stock prices and earnings for companies are down, so what could possibly justify an incentive bonus? The CEO's of Fannie Mae and Freddie Mac received $18 million and $12 million respectively. Both of these firms are Government Sponsored Entities?

Disclosure and accountability need to be addressed for publicly owned companies. They need to make things transparent to investors and the public concerning what they are spending money on, such as ski trips, private jets and sponsoring ball fields. They need to clearly disclose the annual compensation, bonus and incentive guidelines to allow all shareholders the right to review it and vote on it. It is not acceptable for a salaried employee of a major company on the Compensation Committee to decide to award millions of dollars arbitrarily to senior executives of a public company.

If these CEO's are that good, have them take their own money and start a company. Angelo Mozilo did that with Countrywide. He grew that company to the largest in the country and he deserved every single penny he paid himself as the owner of that company. But once he went public with the company and profited handsomely with that public offering, he became an employee of

Countrywide and should have run that company for the benefit of the shareholders. Instead, he controlled his compensation by stealing money that should have gone to the shareholders.

If shareholders do not agree with the company, they can sell the shares and find a company that is working in their best interest. This is the computer age, yet we still receive letters for Proxy Votes. Rarely will you find any that call for more than three things; first, the approval of the accounting firm; second, the election of officers (they give you five choices and ask you to vote for five); and third, they ask you to acknowledge that you agree to let the Board of Directors vote on any other business that comes up.

It's the "other business that comes up" that is stealing money from the shareholders and allowing the executives to use the money as it best suits and benefits them. Some view one of the most stable jobs in a large company as being in a position where you cater to the top executives. The company could be losing huge amounts of money and downsizing employees and selling profitable parts of their company, and these factors are ignored, but when the private chef or the private drivers start getting laid off, the company is in real trouble.

President Obama needs to do for the "Main Street" people. This means addressing the credit crisis immediately. The credit crisis is neither the lack of lending nor the tightening of credit. The true credit crisis is two fold. Consumers are over-extended. But the manner in which consumers are beaten down and destroyed by the credit and collection processes during times of financial hardship is the crux of the credit crisis.

Credit was provided to consumers in a predatory lending manner. Credit cards and lines of credit up to $50,000 were provided to a consumer based on a signature and what is most likely an acceptable credit score. No pay stubs, income verification or anything else to make a sound lending decision for the lender or for the consumer.

Predatory lending practices, such as target marketing through mailings, deceptive marketing through retail stores and continuing to increase credit lines with no justification or verification of ability to pay has adversely affected many consumers. Credit cards charge very high rates for their "unsecured" credit. This is generally acceptable to the average consumer as there is awareness that more risk should carry a higher reward to the lender to offset their potential losses.

When a consumer is unable to make their payments for any reason, such as the horrible economic state the country is in right now, calls are made to the consumer to seek payment. If the consumer is unable to make payments, after several months, that account is sold to a collection agency for a percentage of the face value. A $4,000 past due balance, which may now be $5,000 after late fees, penalties, increased interest rates is sold to a collection agency for $1,000. The lender legally shows the value of that account as $1,000. The lender then legally and accurately writes the other $4,000 off their books as a bad-debt write down.

The consumer now has negative marks on their credit report. This warns others to use caution before lending to them again as they have had difficulty repaying debt in the past. That is another penalty to the consumer for their inability to repay the debt, in addition to the negative credit rating and lower credit scores.

The original lender has balanced their books based on basic accounting principles. The collection agency now has an asset which should be valued at $1,000, the acquisition cost for that asset, plus an applicable interest rate and fees. Here's the catch, the collection agency continues to collect the $5,000 from the consumer. Now without being a mathematician, the $1,000 was paid to the lender by the collection agency; $4,000 was written off by the lender and the $5,000 still being collected somehow now adds up to $9,000. That $4,000 debt has now grown and been manipulated to More than double the initial amount. Not to mention the exorbitant rates which was likely attached. These are Usury numbers regardless of the state definitions.

Collection accounts and charge-offs should be handled the same was as a tax sale certificate. If a home owner falls behind on their property taxes by more than twelve months, the amount of the past due taxes are sold to investors at a fixed rate. Assuming an average interest rate of eighteen percent, an investor may purchase a tax sale certificate for the face value of the balance and penalties and collect the interest on that balance until they are paid in full, often with the sale of the property.

Assuming a $10,000 tax sale certificate, the investor would pay the town, which needs the tax money to operate their budget, and the investor is entitled to the fixed rate interest. The investor cannot charge a higher interest rate and he can not charge more for the payoff than the face value of the certificate. This is a fair way to collect property taxes, which are also a secured lien on real property. How then are credit card balances, supposed unsecured credit, subject to the unreasonable and unfair mathematical calculations?

Instead of giving money to the banks so they can balance their books with base loans, which only helps Wall Street collection agencies, the full $5,000 should be removed from the consumer. This will enable additional cash flow the consumer will spend in the markets in an attempt to increase business revenues, which will increase corporate profits which will allow companies to hire more employees.

The banks end up winning because for whatever period of time the consumers were paying the high interest rates, they made significant income. For the stores that pushed these credit cards on their unsuspecting shoppers, they sold their products, made many sales and increased profits. The collection agencies then bought an undervalued account and not only harassed and haunted the consumers, if they didn't get their money in a timely manner, they sued to collect the full $5,000.

The entire math, reasoning and process do not make any sense at all except for this: The American consumer is a target and is fair game for businesses to abuse and steal from! Most people feel that an unsecured debt is just that, unsecured. If an unsecured account can ultimately become a lawsuit and a judgment, a claim, collection or a wage garnishment against the consumer, that has all the properties of a secured debt. Perhaps a delayed secured account, but secured nonetheless.

In the interest of fair disclosure to consumers, supposedly an important aspect to lending, the disclosure should clearly state in non-legal terms, what it is the consumer is getting themselves into. If the debt is secured, such as a mortgage, car loan, car lease or even a store purchase that may carry a lien on a specific item purchased, so be it. If it is an unsecured debt that will result in numerous harassing calls from commission-based collection agents, only to result in a lawsuit and ultimate payment through the courts for twice the amount of original credit and ultimately destroying the consumer credit profile, resulting in scores causing the consumer to be unable to get good terms on future credit, or unable to get credit at all, then so be it, but disclose it that way.

We must stop banks and lenders from engaging in predatory lending practices by providing Zero Percent credit cards earning bonus miles and points with no annual fees on a card that has been Pre-Approved with no personal information other than what they see on an illegally viewed credit report. Yes, I believe it should be illegal for credit reporting agencies to provide a credit report or even credit scores and personal information such as mailing labels to businesses for the purpose of target marketing.

Let the write offs be a sufficient practice for bad debt. Perhaps lenders will not extend credit to just anyone and sometimes extending credit to animals and the dead. The lenders will be forced to practice sound lending procedures instead of just issuing credit to anyone and everyone. It does not make any sense that collection agencies are permitted to collect on an amount that has been written down legally already. Everyone wins in this scenario except the consumer.

How do we find ourselves here? How do we ever expect to get out of the financial mess we refer to as the U.S. economy?

Spending and deficit conversations referencing Trillions of dollars, with a "T", will burden this country and it's workforce for generations to come.

At a time when unemployment is at very high levels and consumers are losing their homes to foreclosure as they struggle to pay their utility and food bills, government is the only area of employment with rising numbers. Government needs additional workers to help keep track of the bailout money to the banks, insurance companies, automobile industry and everyone else who has their hand for free government money.

Consumers get into trouble with their debts based on the predatory lending practices of banks and lenders in not making sure they can repay the debt. Consumers try to keep up with the neighbors and they want the new cars and big screen televisions. They are lured in with no credit checks, no income verification, no money down and no interest. It seems much too easy and that's because it is.

The lenders always knew what they were doing. They just didn't care. Their only concern was the ability to grow their books so that they could earn their big salaries and ridiculous bonuses. They did this with full knowledge of what they were doing and when it all collapsed, they were bailed out by the government using tax payer money. Annual compensation amounts were often more than average workers would make in several working lifetimes.

The government provided a stimulus package that was intended to put money into the hands of Americans. This added to the deficit but it did not stimulate the economy as planned. Nancy Pelosi wanted this approved to save the country and before they could print the checks she was calling for more spending. Much of that stimulus package went to paying monthly expenses or paying down debt.

They tried to push down interest rates in early 2008, which would have allowed many Americans, most of who were still employed at that time, to refinance and lower their payments, allowing them more flexible cash flow to put back into the economy. Despite the prime lending rate falling, mortgage rates quickly shot up and stayed at disproportionately high levels for much of 2008. This slowed refinances and greatly reduced the home sales which will be the ultimate foothold this country needs to get out of this mess.

With President Barack Obama's stimulus package, the politicians have once again showed their true colors. There is so much pork and fluff in the stimulus package to help their cronies instead of focusing on the problems at hand that the premise of the stimulus is lost. They assume that when you are throwing around trillions of dollars as if it were change dropped on the sidewalk, no one will notice a few billion directed at their pet projects.

How can the American people be expected to demonstrate fiscal responsibility with their finances when the government bears no accountability for their financial actions? California has gone to a four day work week because they are out of money and they have started issuing 'IOU's' as forms of payment. Try sending a letter to your mortgage company with an IOU for a monthly payment. How did that work out for you?

With the government hiring tens of thousands of new employees, we are just getting into a deeper hole. With very few exceptions in the history of the United States, government workers will have a job forever with benefits and retirement payments. The old joke was that a government employee had to kill a person to be fired from their job. That joke is no longer funny because the number of people they need to kill is now three. I don't even think they get written up for just one at this time.

The beneficiary of the bailout money has been the banks. These are the same banks who led us down this dark alley by providing one hundred percent financing on a home with a falsely high value based on the housing bubble. They provided consumers with the financing even though the consumers could not provide proof of income, assets or employment. They allowed the seller to pay closing costs. They allowed the borrower to have a credit profile that had three consumer trade-lines of $500 each for the last three years. To top it all off, they allowed consumers to purchase homes in the range of $650,000 with this criteria. I thought the Wall Street types were supposed to be some of the smartest people in America.

They are absolutely the smartest! I have come to believe that without question. They built this housing bubble by lending money to everyone, including dead people in some instances. They collected great salaries and they collected huge bonuses. When it collapsed, they were not only able to avoid investigation and restitution, but the government gave them more money to cover their exorbitant salaries and their bonuses once again.

By law, all government has to have a balanced budget. This includes federal, state and local government. The problem is that they are allowed to borrow, using future taxes to repay the debt. Because of this, public officials feel there is no bottom to their checking account. The federal government and their deficit is proof of this. How can the average American be expected to demonstrate more financial responsibility than the government and big business?

Executives and senior management of firms see their companies as their own private piggy banks. Only making $20 million a year? Let's get the company to pay for an attorney to renegotiate that contract to $25 million. Take a commercial airline flight? I don't think so; we need a $20 million private jet. I know we are getting public assistance to avoid the company going out of business, but let's commit $400 million ($20 million per year) to name a baseball field after our company. At least they have a private suite with free food and drink to go watch the games because there is no way they are sitting with the poor saps whose money they are stealing to make the deal.

What about when the executives leave the stadium? They may be tired and possibly had a few drinks. No worries for them, they have a car service or a private driver, paid for by company funds.

And to recognize the fact that they were able to write so many one hundred percent no doc loans last year, they get everyone together at a nice expensive resort to say thanks for doing your job.

All of this takes money and that money belongs to the shareholders. I think we have forgotten over the years that the shareholders own the company. The main reason corporate executives have so many shares of stock is that they award themselves huge numbers of shares as incentives every year through bonuses and stock options. While they exercise the options regularly, it is a lot less likely that they took money from their personal accounts and purchased additional shares.

It's time for the government and businesses to be held to the same fiscal responsibilities that the average American is held to. Instead of spending based on anticipated revenues and borrowing against future potential income, spending should be curbed to spending what is already collected and in the account. This is the lesson many Americans are learning through this economic depression. They will limit the amount of credit they use and they will buy the things they need and not necessarily the things they want. This could last for quite some time. There will be a lasting affect on retail stores and manufacturers. The demand for items will become more defined and maybe not every home will have several large screen televisions.

The guidelines for the extension of credit to the consumer need to change. The ramifications and penalties need to be amended. Disclosure to consumers about the credit they are accepting will need to be very clear to distinguish between secured debt and unsecured debt. There will be risks and rewards to lenders and borrowers alike, but at least everyone will go into business together based on full disclosure.

I firmly believe that the United States financial system is under foreign rule. I believe we are still the greatest nation in the world but I have to wonder how things went so wrong with our country. Democrat or Republican, it does not matter. The political machine is broken and has clearly messed things up.

Whether it can be fixed or not is a major question. I'm not a conspiracy theorist. There are things we need to question before it gets too late.

Reality is a wonderful thing, but it is often the perception that matters most. My opinions about a Flat Tax, credit card lenders, Section 8 Housing, Wall Street, the stock market, collection agencies and the economy may not be the same as yours. I can only hope that something will catch your attention and make you ask your own questions and draw your own conclusions.

1

Recession or Depression?

We don't know how history will look back on this current economy. Regardless of how it is labeled by the pundits, it will be different for everyone, based on how it affected them personally. I truly believe it will be labeled as the Depression of 2009!

Near the end of 2008, the U.S. government finally acknowledged not only that we were in a recession, but that we had been in one for nearly a year. Countless politicians and economists consistently told the American people that we were not in a recession.

They continued to explain that a recession had not occurred because there had not been two straight quarters of negative growth. How is it that there is just one statistical measurement of whether the economy is in a recession?

With all of the drastic changes in America and the world, how is it possible to be able to so simply define the criteria for a recession? There are many more people in the world than in years before. There are more illegal immigrants in the United States, some recognized and some not. There are many people working off the books. It has become a world economy, with computers and out-sourcing moving functions and capacities from inside our borders to other countries.

Things have changed and the government has refused to acknowledge that. Or, more likely, they knew, but they were just denying the fact so that the American people would not have even more bad news to hear. Unless we believe our government does not recognize basic economics, I think it's evident that the government knew we were in a recession. They were just hoping that the recession would pass quickly enough so that they could acknowledge the recession in past tense. Hope is not a strategy and timing did not work out well for them with this one.

One of the key reasons to believe the government knew about the recession was when they lowered the fed funds rate by 75 basis points in an emergency fed meeting in very early 2008. The lowering of the fed funds rate is a normal catalyst for other interest rates to follow suit and this includes mortgage rates.

The day they dropped the federal funds rate by that huge amount, the markets reacted and the mortgage rates dropped. This brought the rates down to the 5.5% range. The government believed this would help stimulate mortgage activity and as a result, housing would have an opportunity to recover.

The concept of leveraging lower mortgage rates to aid in the recovery of the overall economy is a correct move. Housing drives a good part of the economy. With lower mortgage rates, there are a number of positive results that can occur.

There is a mortgage industry estimate that says: For every eighth (.125%) that the rates move (up or down) that many more potential buyers are either in or out of the market to buy a home. This is based on the psychological number potential home buyers are looking for.

If homes have come down in price, the borrower has a good job, some money for a down payment and an overall positive feeling of their personal situation; they will have a target rate in their head that says it is time to jump into the market to look at homes.

Unfortunately, when they dropped the fed funds rate by such a large percentage in a special meeting before a regularly scheduled meeting, they spooked the overall economy. Not only did the rates immediately start going back up, but they went to over 7.00% during the summer months. This, combined with steadily declining home prices and growing unemployment numbers, had caused a great number of potential borrowers to flee from the market.

As the mortgage rates go down, homeowners have more options to achieve their financial goals and objectives. A refinance to lower their monthly payment will not only make them more comfortable, but it could provide additional funds to set aside to avoid future issues. They can also refinance to pay off other consumer debt to lower their monthly obligations. While this can help cash flow, it will almost certainly end up costing the consumer more in the long run.

Options are there for consumers. In addition to 30 year fixed rates, there are also 15 year, 20 year and 25 year term loans to consider. This gives consumers the option to balance monthly payments against total interest costs.

With extra funds in their cash flow, money will be available for additional purchases, which can help the retail numbers. This is "extra money" at that time for the consumers. The consumer was just paying their bills, but by lowering the payment, they now have additional discretionary funds.

A $250 per month payment reduction is a net amount. The consumer has already paid taxes on that money. They needed to earn $300 per month in order to get that $250 in their account. That is a $3,600 gross income savings for the consumer. That's just like getting a $3,600 raise and at this time when many companies are laying off tremendous numbers of workers; a $3,600 raise is a huge difference.

Volatility in the interest rates has kept many potential buyers on the side lines. Even with continuing weakness in home prices, they have come down enough that first time home buyers see an opportunity to buy cheap. Even if the property value drops another five to ten percent in the next six to twelve months, the home is more than an investment, it's their primary residence. It comes with the special benefits of pride of ownership, building equity, no landlord to deal with and other positive and personal reasons a buyer wants to own a home.

The interest rate volatility is keeping many potential buyers waiting. They can call any given day at eleven in the morning when rates are normally established for the day and get the current rate. By the afternoon, there is a chance that the rates have changed at least once and sometimes several times in any given day. This volatility impacts the credibility of mortgage loan officers and originators.

When first time home buyers finally enter the market, they will most likely be looking for average priced existing homes. The sellers of these homes will then become buyers of other homes, either existing or possibly new homes. New homes tend to be higher priced and that is the reason most buyers purchase existing homes first.

This concept of seller becoming buyer is what will get the market moving again. Unfortunately, statistics show that there are huge jumps in foreclosure home sales, especially in certain areas such as California, Las Vegas and Florida. These are not true sales of families buying homes. The foreclosed properties are mostly sold to investors who happen to have the financial liquidity that it takes to purchase these homes, either as investment properties or to make repairs and then put back on the market for sale at a future date.

When the housing market does stabilize, and it will, it will be the starting point for the overall economic recovery. As homes sell, there are normally Realtors involved. Most homes are not sold for cash so there is a mortgage lender and a final investor for the home mortgage loan. For a purchase there are normally two attorneys, a title company, a home owner's insurance agent, an appraiser and a home inspector that will earn income on that transaction.

Others that benefit from purchase transactions are the moving companies; painters and paint manufacturers as new owners clean and paint their new home; furniture stores; carpeting; home products and so many other retail stores, wholesalers; manufacturers and raw material suppliers.

Housing starts the economic recovery. Whether it is a purchase or a refinance, both benefit the consumer and the overall economy. It is ridiculous to throw billions and even trillions of dollars to the banking institutions. These are the same banking institutions that put the American people into this mess. They are using the money to shore up their balance sheets, pay their dividends and bonuses and even use the money to purchase other struggling banks is ridiculous.

Wall Street continues to try to pick out any possible bit of good news. Over the past year, many analysts and "experts" have stated that the bottom of the market had been hit. These "guesses" continue to benefit the person making the statements as they can be seen as steering consumers through deception. Stock traders, who get paid to make transactions, want market movement to make sure they can continue to buy and sell stocks so that they can get paid.

The stock traders don't actually own most of the stocks they are trading and they do not care if the stock goes up in value or not. The analysts that continue to pick the stocks that are outperforming the world and their picks are where everyone should be. If you notice the disclosures on the television when these analysts are making their picks, they very rarely own that stock themselves in any manner.

Analysts with conflicting opinions are alternated and sometimes on the screen at the same time. Who do you believe? How much do you believe them? Regardless of your personal opinion, people make financial decisions because of what they hear. People take action and buy a stock. Buying a stock pushes the price up. The better the stock market does, the better the news on television, in the papers and online.

When there is good news, there is higher consumer confidence. With higher consumer confidence comes more spending and with more spending comes more borrowing. And once again we fall into the vicious cycle until the "Boom and Bust" forces determine which area of the economy will pay the price next. It's never pretty, and it always impacts the individual in the form of pain and suffering.

This is not "normal market movement"; this is well calculated and planned economic growth and economic contraction. The results are pain and suffering for many for the profitability of the few. The spread between the "Haves and Have-Nots" continues to grow, year after year, decade after decade. We all want better for our children, but the obstacles continue to grow.

2

Fannie Mae and Freddie Mac

The government made an attempt in early 2008 to lower the federal funds rate to push mortgage rates down. However, as of January 2009 they have failed to utilize their strongest tool to control the mortgage rates for the benefit of the home buyers, home owners and economic consumers, overall.

Many families will lose their homes because they have lost their jobs or fallen behind because of rising interest rate adjustments, higher energy costs and other financial factors.

On September 8, 2008 the U.S. government took over Fannie Mae (FNMA - Federal National Mortgage Association) and Freddie Mac (FHLMC- Federal Home Loan Mortgage Corporation). These are both GSE's (Government Sponsored Entities), which means they are supposedly private for-profit corporations, that have the implied support and backing of the U.S. Government.

When the government took over Fannie Mae and Freddie Mac that implied backing became a very specific and definite backing. Fannie Mae and Freddie Mac own or control approximately $12 trillion in outstanding mortgage debt in the United States.

It's not difficult to determine what went wrong at Fannie Mae and Freddie Mac. In 2007, Fannie Mae CEO Daniel Mudd had an $11.6 million salary with stock and other compensation.

Freddie Mac CEO Richard Syron made $18.3 million in 2007. He also received a car and a driver, a home security system, travel costs for his wife, and $100,000 to pay his lawyer to renegotiate his employment contract.

That is certainly a lot of income for two men to run these government-sponsored-entities into the ground. There are plenty of other potential executives that could have managed these companies into the ground, possibly not even as severely, for significantly less money. These are large companies and I am not saying that the CEO's of companies this size don't deserve to make a good amount of money. But what is the level of compensation before it becomes absolutely ridiculous?

Just the point six and the point three after the millions in their salaries would have enabled them to hire educated, hard working and honest CEO's for those positions. Those simple decimal points would still have placed them in the top two percent of compensation for individuals in the country.

These two CEO's earned more than $30 million in 2007. How many mortgage loans have to be securitized to earn that type of income? This is before you account for a single penny of what other employees made, the cost of the operations centers, computers and supplies. Let us not forget about the investors that put money into the stock of that company in hopes of getting a positive return. Instead, that money went straight into the pockets of these senior managers that should be ashamed of themselves.

Where is the accountability? These CEO's have made millions upon millions and with a good number of people losing their homes; they are sitting back care-free and without recourse. Something is very wrong with this picture.

These CEO's were no better than the big securities traders from Wall Street. They knew that they were slicing and dicing up bad loans to put into pools to sell as collateralized debt obligations and cross-collateralized securities. They continued to do more and more to make sure their numbers increased so that their bonuses would continue as long as possible.

When it hit the fan for Fannie Mae and Freddie Mac, they started losing their investors. American and foreign investors realized the house of cards was collapsing and they pulled their money out. To continue lending and paying the CEO salaries, they needed to increase capital. That required that they sell bonds priced higher than treasury market prices. This caused mortgage bonds to go up, even as the treasury prices were going down. This totally undermined the goal and objective of the U.S. government to lower interest rates.

One primary negative result of the Fannie Mae and Freddie Mac problems has been the pricing adjustments based on risk factors. Until recently, the price of a 30 year mortgage loan was the same with few adjustments. This presumes the credit score was under a 620, if it was an investment property or if the owner was taking additional cash out of the property over 70% of the value.

The current pricing grid reflects a risk-based model never seen before. There are negative pricing adjustments for scores that are over 740. They are squeezing and picking at every borrower to get a little more. And it's not always a little more. For example, assume a borrower has a mid score between 620 to a 639 and they are buying or refinancing a home at 75% loan to value. That's 25% down, a pretty good feeling that they intend to make the payments and a limited level of risk should they go into default. The pricing adjustment is equal to three points. Each point is one percent of the loan amount, so it would be $3,000 for a $300,000 loan. Fannie Mae and Freddie Mac are making these borrowers pay an additional $9,000 for that loan.

That makes the financing cost prohibitive for many consumers. Assuming that home owner had a mortgage at almost seven percent, perhaps from a purchase at the high point of 2008, and the current rates are at five percent, the borrower would have to pay not only the closing costs for the new loan, but at least those three points, making the break even period too long and the refinance would be unjustified. That $300 a month they could have been saving will not help them pay down other debt nor will it be spent in the economy on other things to help the American economy recover.

The U.S. government should be using their powers and their direct control of Fannie Mae and Freddie Mac to help American consumers. The underwriting criteria have changed several times over the last few months. They are being more careful in reviewing information. They are verifying income on every borrower. They are doing more diligent searches to make sure the information in the file is accurate. Bottom line, NOW they are doing good loans.

Many financial news programs are reporting that there are no mortgages available to a buyer. However, that is not true. Some are saying that you need 20% down to buy a home, and that's not true. They are saying it's more difficult to get financing. That is actually true; but not a bad thing. Borrowers that can document and demonstrate they can repay the debt, CAN get financing.

The actual rate and terms will vary based on how good the credit score is. While generally a good indicator, there are many problems with the reliance we have on the credit reporting agencies and the way they do business. This can affect consumers and either make it more expensive for them to borrow or eliminate them for meeting the more restrictive criteria.

There are mortgage insurance companies available to assist borrowers that meet the underwriting criteria but who have a low down payment. There are some conventional investors that will finance five percent down but others that require a larger down payment. This is based on states and areas being in what are called a "declining market area", such as most of New Jersey at this time. The FHA (Federal Housing Administration) program still only requires a three and a half percent down payment.

Because of these new requirements and guidelines, it has made it even more important to have a mortgage pre-approval done with a lender. We make sure that the credit scores, income ratios and all other aspects of the file meet the requirements of what will be required for the estimated home price of the potential purchase.

This provides the consumer with the information they need to make prudent choices and it also provides the Realtors, attorneys and the home sellers with a comfort level that the potential buyer will be able to purchase the home when they go into contract. Potential home buyers should never pay any up front fees for this service. If the mortgage professional requires you pay for this customer service, find another lender.

Government use of Fannie Mae Freddie Mac can get the economy moving and get many of the so-called toxic loans removed. As an existing mortgage is refinanced at this time, it will be removed from the toxic category and placed into a new, better and improved loan category because it was originated after January 1, 2009. The existing mortgage was paying on time, there was equity in the property and the consumer met all underwriting guidelines. The fact that it was pre-existing through the crisis is why it was labeled toxic.

The goal is to provide not only rates that are beneficial for the borrower, but make rates somewhat stable. Limit the fluctuations in pricing, not only from day to day, but over the course of a day. Small adjustments based on other market movements, but the government can stabilize the rates and allow the refinances to happen. President Obama's stimulus plan includes subsidizing payments for "at risk" owners. That money should have been used to subsidize lower rates for everyone instead of for the very small percentage of owners that will be able to benefit from it.

As the loans refinance, the toxic loans will be paid off. This will free up the balance sheets of the banks holding the loans, Fannie Mae and Freddie Mac included. Reducing the pricing adjustments will make it more beneficial for all borrowers to refinance. A borrower who missed a credit card payment when they were on vacation three years ago is not a risky loan. This is especially true when you have reviewed their income, assets and liabilities and done a full appraisal and possibly a desk review or two to make sure the value of the home is there.

Fannie Mae and Freddie Mac accepted loans that did not verify income for a long time. They called it full documentation. They conformed to the automated underwriting system that the borrower had full documentation to support the income put into the system. However, the only requirement was a verbal verification and the actual documentation was not required as part of the file. For borrowers with good credit, that was a "stated income loan", at full documentation pricing, thanks to Fannie Mae and Freddie Mac themselves.

Fannie Mae and Freddie Mac need to get back to doing stated income loans. They just need to do it the correct way. There are many self-employed and commissioned borrowers that have tax returns that do not truly support their income amount. They are utilizing the allowable tax deductions to lower their tax burdens. This is allowed by the IRS, and their Adjusted Gross Income on their federal tax returns does not come close to the actual income amount.

The long-standing philosophy has always understood that this to be the case for these types of borrowers, which was the original purpose of the stated income product. It had to make sense. A self-employed plumber with $300,000 in the bank could state he made $15,000 a month as long as there was good credit behind it. This actually makes sense. The overall profile and picture of this borrower is good. The risk is minimal.

The problems began when the Wall Street Investors, Fannie Mae and Freddie Mac and others started offering even more aggressive financing to borrowers. Remember, their executives needed to hit certain numbers to get their big bonuses. If they needed to put people in homes they could not afford, then so be it. But do not think for a second, that they were going to accept NOT reaching their goals and NOT getting their bonuses.

Mortgage programs were developed that allowed borrowers to state their income up to very high levels, even 100% and sometimes higher, so they could finance their closing costs. The underwriting criteria and guidelines were so insufficient on these loans that it was clearly a matter of time before they all collapsed.

A sample loan would be a borrower that claims to make $12,000 a month. They have no housing history because they previously lived at home with their parents. They need 100% financing because they have no money. They are getting a three percent seller concession from the seller, which probably means the house appraisal is already over-valued, and they need a gift from their parents to establish the escrow accounts. The borrower has three small credit cards for $1,000 or less on each for three years and the new home is $400,000, taxes of $800 per month and the monthly payment will be about $4,000 per month. The borrower has an 800 credit score.

All of these items, while not great, would actually meet the guidelines for a 100% financing program. The monthly payment of $4,000 is only thirty three percent of the gross income, which is stated, not verified or documented. Don't forget that part. The debts are all small, so they don't really affect the qualifying ratios. Going from a zero housing payment to $4,000 per month is not great, but that also is not a reason for denial. Everything is acceptable to an underwriter that is going through a checklist. It's acceptable to the wholesaler that is closing the loan and who will be shipping off the loan to the final investor.

The lender selling the loan is normally on the hook for four to six months. That means they are hoping that the client makes the monthly payments, somehow, someway, until they are no longer on the hook for the loan. Some lenders actually followed up with the consumers after the loan was sold, to make sure they borrowed the money from relatives to make sure the payments were made for those few months. Some lenders would actually help pay the mortgage payments to avoid a potential recapture of that loan and income. This was a practice forbidden in most contracts.

After the first few months, the recourse is gone and they have nothing to worry about. The problem with this is that it was acceptable and common. They tried hard to find reasons to do loans, based on being pressured to make housing available and affordable to all, but there was something missing about many of the loans being closed. The thing missing was common sense.

Common sense and life experiences are two important tools for an underwriter. Anyone can check off a bank statement, a credit report, an appraisal and all other required items in a file.

The one piece of information left out of the summary of the borrower is that with all that other info, the $12,000 per month was derived from working in a fast food restaurant for two years. Not as the owner of the restaurant and often not even the manager. They were saying that the person that takes your order and hands you your food was claiming to make $12,000 per month. This is where common sense had to come into play. This is $2,769 per week. Assuming a salary of $20 per hour for this employee, they would have had to work 138 hours a week to earn that gross income. That is over nineteen hours a day, seven days a week. It should have at least prompted a few more questions.

Loans like this should never have been done. Questions should have been asked and additional information should have been requested. This was often a borrower that wanted to take advantage of the sky-rocketing housing market. They figured the closing costs were paid for and there was no down payment. They thought they could turn around in several months and sell it for a profit. We all know where that got us.

3

Credit Card Lenders
Usury & RICO

Companies that issue credit cards should be charged and prosecuted for the crimes they commit against the American consumer. They are in violation of usury laws and RICO.

Usury laws are state laws that specify the maximum legal interest rate that loans can charge. The act of receiving more than the principle lent is called "interest" for anyone who believes that lending money and charging interest is legal and it is called "usury" by those that don't.

Each state specifies what they consider to be the maximum legal interest rate. In Delaware, the legal interest rate is 5% over the Federal Reserve Rate. In Illinois the legal rate of interest is 5% and the usury limit and judgment rate is 9%. In Michigan the legal interest rate is 5%, the general usury rate is 7% and judgments bear interest at a rate of 1% above the five year Treasury note rate.

In the District of Columbia the legal interest rate is 6% and the general usury limit is in excess of 24%. In South Dakota the legal rate of interest is 15%, judgments are at a rate of 12% and there is no usury rate. It's very hard to be guilty of lending money at an interest rate more than two times the local state usury rate when there is no established usury rate. Citi, Citbank, Citigroup, whatever you would like to call them, is based in South Dakota. That is not surprising in any way.

RICO is the Racketeer Influenced and Corrupt Organizations Act. This is a federal law that provides for extended criminal and civil penalties for acts that are performed on behalf of an ongoing criminal organization. Originally designed to crack down on the Mafia, RICO laws clearly need to concentrate some effort on the credit card lenders.

Under RICO guidelines, a person that is a member of an enterprise that has committed two crimes from a list of 35 crimes, of which 27 are federal and 8 are state, in a 10-year period can be charged with racketeering. Top executives and senior managers at the credit card companies should sit up and take note because the next knock on their door may be a RICO subpoena with their name on it.

The penalties for racketeering are fines up to $25,000 and a prison term up to 20 years. In addition, they must forfeit all of their gains and profits from any business through a pattern of "racketeering activity".

RICO also allows a private individual that is harmed by such activity to file a civil suit and, if successful, they can collect treble damages. Treble damages are a precedent that allows the court to triple the amount of the damages as a form of punishment to the guilty party.

Not only should the executives and senior managers at the credit card companies be afraid, any and all investors that own stock in these companies should also take note. When these civil suits start, the penalties will destroy the companies, and the shareholders will lose their investments.

An interesting fact about RICO-related charges is that they are somewhat easy to prove in court, as it focuses on consistent behavior on behalf of the guilty parties.

A pattern of racketeering would require at least two acts of racketeering activity. The credit card companies are clearly guilty of more than just two of the qualifying actions and any credit card company that is still is business at this time has committed these crimes after the RICO guidelines went into effect and the actions have occurred within the last 10 years.

The following acts prove that credit card companies are guilty of racketeering and are therefore in violation of RICO laws:

Bribery is the first action of the credit card companies. Credit card companies secretly hide their true identities and issue credit to unknowing consumers through store cards of popular retail stores. The credit card companies then bribe the retail stores to push their credit card accounts to the consumers with specials such as a discount on their first purchase or some other incentive.

The consumer believes they are doing business with the store. The store is only a front for the credit card lender to push themselves into the wallet of the consumer. The credit card companies know that the minimum payment and the initial discount will hook the consumer and they also know most people will not pay off the balance and the card will continue to accrue interest, thus earning the credit card company big profits.

The deception of having the consumer believe they obtained credit from the retail store is also fraud. The name on the card is not the name of the true lender; it is the name of the retail store where the employee and employer were compensated to encourage the consumer to obtain additional credit from a third party.

The combined efforts of the retail store and the credit card lender in these carefully orchestrated activities to overwhelm consumers with additional debt, is racketeering. Whether it is a percent off the first purchase or a 30 day grace period with no interest, the consumer is carefully manipulated and ends up a victim of steering, coercion and predatory lending practices.

Credit card companies are also guilty of securities fraud. They obtain minimal information about the unsuspecting consumer, have a credit report run to determine their credit score and get basic information from the consumer. None of that information is even validated. There is no analysis of whether the consumer is over-extended or if this credit may cause financial hardship on the consumer. They then market their profitability to investors as valid lending to encourage investments.

The credit card companies are clearly guilty of violating RICO guidelines for racketeering. It is a carefully thought out process to take advantage of the consumer and entrap them into a vicious cycle of financial hardship.

Since states get to set different acceptable usury rates for Americans only proves that the corruption in government is at different levels in different locations in the country. On such an important issue, maximum lending rates, why would the Federal Government not regulate and control it better? It's rather obvious, it is designed to reward the wealthy and take advantage of the lower and middle classes.

How are usury rates set? How could the usury rate in New Jersey be six times that of the legal lending rate? Wouldn't a legal lending rate of 6% make anything over that an illegal lending rate?

Late Fees and Over-Limit Fees should also be calculated into the determination of usury. If a payment is several days late, there is a penalty. If you make a purchase and when combined with the accrued interest charges it makes you go over your line of credit limit, there is a penalty. These fees should also be considered when making the calculations because simple interest is based on the actual number of days. A $35 penalty when the daily accrued interest is less than a few dollars is nothing more than taking advantage of the consumer.

In 1980, due to the high level of inflation, the federal government changed the rules for national banks and federally chartered savings banks. They can ignore state usury limits and set their interest rates a specific amount higher than the Federal Reserve discount rate. On December 16, 2008 they lowered the Discount rate from 1.00% to a range of 0.00% to 0.25%. Take a look at your credit cards and see what interest rates you are still paying on your cards. In New Jersey it is probably between 10 and 24% higher than the discount rate.

The government has done nothing to protect the consumer. The credit card lenders are nothing more than a cartel of thieves preying on the American consumer.

4

Ultimate Greed

The United States does not control its own financial system or economy. That privilege belongs to the Federal Reserve, which is owned and operated by private foreign entities. The majority of the world's wealth is controlled by these private foreign entities.

If they want the stock market to go to 12,000, it's going to 12,000. If they want the 10 year treasury at 2.00%, it will get there. If they want houses to go up in value or for commercial properties to increase in value, it's done.

The Stock Market Crash of 1929 was a carefully planned and executed event. The market was going up day after day. The stock market was driven up and without warning to anyone except the inner circle of the super wealthy; the stocks were sold at huge profits, taking the inflated profits from all the investors with it. The average person never saw it coming. Stock brokers and even the semi-wealthy were caught by surprise.

People lost their life savings. Businesses, including banks, went out of business, making the existing banks even stronger. As companies went out of business, people lost their jobs and ultimately their homes. The homes were foreclosed by the banks that had extended them the credit to buy the homes. Without jobs and without money, this carefully planned crisis made the wealthy even wealthier.

This same group of wealth cartel has done this repeatedly and continues to bleed America dry. Housing prices more than doubled in a few short years. Alan Greenspan, Federal Reserve

Chairman from 1987 to 2006 is the person most responsible for the current housing crisis. Greenspan pushed for more opportunities for potential home-buyers. He wanted more programs to allow immigrants and skilled workers to buy homes.

Alan Greenspan was working on behalf of the Federal Reserve Bank as the Federal Reserve Chairman. He pushed for the less restrictive guidelines and the lower interest rates as a way to make people homeowners. The more potential buyers, the more demand for the specific quantity of homes. The more demand, the higher the values. The higher the values, the more it appeared people had achieved a level of wealth that allowed them to purchase large ticket items such as furniture and big screen televisions for their new homes.

What Greenspan was truly doing was working for the international cartel that runs the American banking system through the illegal organization known as the Federal Reserve. Greenspan's plan was to grow the housing values to such levels that consumers would consistently have to borrow against any equity available.

As there was more money made available, consumers spent more. This allowed retail stores to prosper, which led to increased profits for wholesalers and manufacturers. There was plenty of work as the Gross Domestic Product was growing at an unprecedented and unjustified pace. The stock market was rallying as the businesses were doing so well. Dividends were being paid and everyone had extra money that they now wanted to invest. Where did people invest their money? In the stock market!

Let's fast forward to recent history. What happened is that we have been led to the edge of the cliff and pushed off. The rug has been pulled right out from underneath us as we were feeling great about our financial positions and our futures. We did not complain about the little things, like the high interest rates on the credit cards because things were good. That's not the case for most people now.

This was a very specific plan of action. The banks now foreclose on the homes and we know who owns the banks, the Federal Reserve. As homeowners miss a mortgage payment, many lenders are sending appraisers out to the homes to determine the condition and the estimated value of the property. If the home is worth less than the mortgage loan, which is the case for many of the owners that purchased homes in the last few years, with no down payment and no ability to pay, the lenders are pushing them to the side to worry about them later. They don't want to bring more bad loans to the front of the pile; they anticipate dealing with them later when times are better.

For the homeowners that may have been in their homes for many years, having built a good amount of equity in the home, things are different. They may be a victim of circumstance and be unemployed from their long time job, or had other cash flow issues. When the lender sees that there is equity in the property, they see a profitable foreclosure. They then proceed as quickly as possible. The borrowers that have made payments over many years are the ones that will suffer the most. This is another example of how the collateral damage of this economy is very often punishing the consumers that deserved it the least.

5

Securing America:
Improving Borrowing and Lending

The current practice of "unsecured debt" in the United States has to be changed before it destroys any more consumers, families and ultimately the entire economy of the United States.

That may seem like a very bold statement, especially since you are probably thinking that consumer debt is not that important. Consumer debt is available everywhere. The stores like Sears, Macys and Kohls will actually give you an immediate discount on a purchase to open a store card. There are Visa, MasterCard, Discover and American Express applications in most restaurants, supermarkets, diners and convenience stores.

The "Pre-Approved" credit card applications you receive at your home can be a regular part of your daily mail. If you fall into the right category, the credit bureaus are providing your information to these credit card companies for a fee. They then begin an aggressive target marketing campaign on you until the timing is right and you can use extra cash flow. Then you get their card.

Now they have you! You are the proverbial moth and you've ended up in their web. They are the spider of course. They may not kill you right now...but give them time. The reason for their aggressive marketing is because we as consumers try to be smarter than this. We are barely getting by on our income with the other expenses we have to live. While having access to these funds will allow us to access something we could not otherwise afford, at some point in time, after having that "pre-approved" mailing there for you to access, you finally throw caution to the wind and get the card.

"It's only a $1,000 credit line and I am only going to need to use $100 and that's only a $10 payment each month." No big deal, you can carry that for a few months and when you get a raise, work some overtime, win the lottery or inherit some money, you can pay it off with no harm and no foul.

While that is a great plan, what happens in reality is that the consumer finds other ways to utilize the full credit line. Maybe they need new tires on their car or an insurance payment is due and money is tight…so those expenses go on the credit card. As they approach an $800 balance and they are now making payments of $40 a month, they realize they are running out of credit and will need to access more credit to pay for food next month. They send in another application and get another credit card for $1,000.

When the first credit card company sees you have been paying your bill on time, albeit using credit to do so, and they see that you have opened another credit card, they go ahead and extend their credit limit to you to $2,500. This will keep you, as the other card is only $1,000 and you would not want to close a card with the higher credit limit. You never know if you will need the additional funds in a pinch.

Well, that so called "pinch" becomes living expenses such as food, gas and utilities. Through the magic of compounding interest and probably some well planned and executed late fees, overdraft charges and cash-advance costs, your credit cards are soon maxed out. Now what?

What happens next is where you realize there is no such thing as unsecured debt. They sell it as such to justify the usury (in layman's terms this means outrageously high and predatory that should be considered illegal in modern society) interest rates and fees.

We were raised that debt has to be prioritized. Taking a mortgage loan is acknowledging a lien on your home that you realize if you don't pay, you can lose your home. That's called a foreclosure. Car loans are specific loans for that specific car. If you don't pay your car loan, they come and take your car back. That's called repossession. These are both well known to most consumers.

Loans appear to be priced to relate to relative risk. Mortgages are normally low, as they know they can take back the home, known as the collateral, if they don't receive their payments. There are risks associated with this, as the value of the home could go down, the home may be damaged or in need of other repairs and it can take a long time to go through the legal process to actually get to foreclose on the home. That's understood by the lender and the consumer. The consumer will have the derogatory payment history on their credit report, ultimately showing a foreclosure, and the lender takes the home back.

Auto loans are similar. If you fall behind far enough on the payments, the lender will repossess the vehicle. They will pay someone to come and take the vehicle from you, whether it is in the middle of the night from your home or while you are shopping at the grocery store with your children. It's understood by the consumer that the car is the collateral for that car loan and this is the result of not paying the car payment. Auto loans vary in rate, but are normally close to the rates of a mortgage loan, depending on whether the vehicle is new or used.

Until several years ago, mortgage loans were provided to consumers with the ability and willingness to repay the debt. Their income, assets, liabilities and credit history were scrutinized. This ensured that the lender was giving money to a consumer and that the consumer would have the means to pay it back. The risk is that something changes in the consumer's life, such as the loss of a job and income, or the death of a borrower and the loss of that income to the family, a medical issue or potentially other life-changing events. The bottom line for underwriting had always been to make a sound lending decision and to make a reasonable assessment of the potential borrower. Otherwise, the loan was denied.

Unsecured debt takes us in an entirely different direction as related to lending. The credit card companies "target", yes, that's right, they target as in hunters going after their prey, consumers that they determine will utilize their credit cards to make purchases. Whether it is a high end purchase of furniture for thousands of dollars or numerous small purchases to put food on the table for their families, they have been targeted as needing more money than they have and earn.

The credit card offers are relentless in their pursuit of the consumer needing extra money. They send the pre-approved offers over and over again until their timing is just right. Now starts the pain and suffering. Send in a late payment and suddenly you have the minimum payments for two months as well as the late payment fee. This can be the start of a vicious cycle of problems, pain and suffering.

The calls from the credit card companies are aggressive from the start. They want you to make a payment by telephone that day or even post-date a check. If you do not have any money in your account now, and you are not sure what you will have in the account in the next two weeks, why would anyone write a post-dated check? If that check or any other check bounces, you are looking at significant fees and charges for that situation.

If a payment can't be made for a few months, the account will be sold to a collection agency. This is where the credit card company takes your $1,000 balance, sells it to a third party for $200, writes off the $800 on their books as a bad debt, and then they wipe their hands of you as a client and a debtor as their books are balanced.

How a $1,000 debt gets sold for $200 and the debt collector has the right to collect on the initial amount of $1,000 is not quite clear. That same $1,000 is written down as any other business expense, for $800 and sold for $200. That clearly makes the value of that debt $200 going forward. How can it be valued at anything different? But they continue to pursue collection efforts to collect the $1,000. That would indicate that the value of this $1,000 debt is actually $1,800 as the initial credit card issuer legally wrote off $800 already.

By this time they have destroyed your credit report. The initial creditor, who lent you the money as "unsecured" at a very high interest rate, damaged your credit when you could not pay and they wrote down the debt.

Debt collection is a huge business and they are collecting amounts on debts that do not exist. In this example, they purchased an account receivable for $200. The other $800 was written off by the initial creditor.

If they want to purchase that $1,000, at the prevailing interest rate that the credit card was issued, then they have the right to collect on the full $1,000. That makes sense as the original creditor was paid $1,000 for that account and they did not take a write off on their books for any loss. It should be clearly disclosed and documented what the acquisition cost is to establish the value of the debt to the collection agency.

If you were to purchase a used car from a dealer, that had a blue book value of $10,000, yet they were willing to take $7,000 for that vehicle, what is your cost basis? It's $7,000 because that is what you paid for it. If you purchased that vehicle for business purposes and you wrote off the amount of $10,000 because that was the value of the vehicle, even though you only paid $7,000 for it, the numbers would not be accurate and it would not make sense. There is no reason that the purchase of the credit card debt is any different.

The unsecured part of the unsecured credit card industry is a farce. You will be harassed and threatened by mail and telephone. The collection agencies will then pursue any means necessary and often illegal means, to collect on the debt. This can result in collections, judgments, pay garnishments and even liens on your home.

How does an unsecured debt, marketed as an unsecured credit card, evolve into a secured lien? You pay higher interest rates for the time you have the card and make payments, which can be for many years. The higher interest rates have been brain-washed into our heads as "risk based" since it is an unsecured credit card and a certain percentage of credit cards will go into default. When due diligence is not performed, lending decisions are not sound. When credit is extended to a consumer who may or may not be able to repay the debt, delinquencies are bound to happen.

You paid ridiculous fees for late charges and over-limit fees. There are countless reports of credit card companies posting payments later in a day after the debits to make it appear you went over your limit, justifying a large fee. You may also make a small purchase that puts you over your limit by just a few dollars; to later find out they charged you $39 for that convenience.

You had your credit rating affected by the credit card company, showing the late payments when you fell behind and could not catch up. The collection agencies, of which there could be several that work on your account over the next few months, list their collections on the credit as a public record and derogatory credit in addition to the initial credit lender.

You'll pay now with the stress and pain and panic of the situation as you fall behind. You'll pay emotionally as you get call after call from callous collectors that could not give a crap about you. They call and tell you they want to help. What they want to help is their own income as they attempt to collect a debt much higher than should actually exist, resulting in a huge and what should be an illegal margin.

All of this will ultimately end up with a collection, judgment, garnishment or a lien which from the perspective of any reasonable human being, will be seen as a secured lien. OK, maybe we can see it as a "delayed secured" lien, but if it is going to be paid one way or the other, then it has to be considered a secured lien and not the unsecured credit perceived by the consumers or as it is sold by the lenders.

The result from this is that lenders will not lend to you. And if they do, it will end up costing you much more money as the perceived risk is higher. This will be true for every type of credit for years and years to come.

America needs to go to a truly secured credit industry. In addition to mortgages and auto loans being secured by very specific items, all credit should be secured. The optimal situation would be to have every credit card actually be a debit card from the checking account or have the credit limit of a card secured for that account.

Every consumer would be allowed a maximum of three credit cards at any given time, with a combined credit limit determined by their actual ability to repay. Consumers could shop cards but would have to close one to open another, so as not to over-extend their debts and cause financial problems, family stress, emotional suffering and unnecessary bankruptcies and collection efforts.

In addition, for true credit related limits, every transaction would specifically secure real property. Credit can not be used to purchase food or gasoline. A secured card or debit card, and perhaps even cash would be needed.

When a television set is purchased, that amount is specifically earmarked for that item and it is knowingly secured for that amount of credit. A television, stereo or even patio furniture would be the secured part of that credit line. If the payments are not made, those items will be repossessed. If those items are not returned, even if they have broken and been discarded, then the amount would become an immediate collection item with the creditor able to attach judgments or liens on the consumer.

The reason that this is OK is that the consumer will knowingly be going into the transaction knowing that the transaction is "secured". Knowing that the item is being secured is the key. Finding out months or years later that unsecured and secured mean entirely different things to the real world but learning that in credit card finance they are the same, just with different timing, is absolutely horrible and it will continue to cause damage to the economy.

As more consumers learn this, their credit is destroyed. As more consumers have their credit history and scores destroyed, they become less likely to purchase a home. As they become less likely to buy a home, they cause fewer buyers to be in the market, which causes home prices to not appreciate as much as possible. As home prices suffer, less people buy homes (welcome to 2008).

As homes don't sell, Realtors, mortgage companies, real estate attorneys, homeowners' insurance agents, movers and title companies, among others, have less business. There are less new home-owners buying paint for their new homes. There are less new home-owners buying refrigerators, washers, dryers, beds, other furniture, etc.

And thus we find ourselves in the Depression of 2009. A depression based on the horrible financial and housing markets and the depressed consumers that did whatever they could to get through this horrific time. At the same time, the CEO's of major firms on Wall Street were running their companies into the ground while making multi-million dollar salaries and compensation packages.

6

Demise of the Middle Class

The Depression of 2009 will be the demise of the middle class. The hard-working, tax-paying citizens are paying a terrible price during this horrible financial crisis and the results will be devastating for many years to come.

The middle class is the most heavily burdened by taxes. They are not the "takers" or the "privileged". The takers are the Section 8 Housing, welfare, free health coverage, food stamp recipients and the abusers of unemployment benefits. This also includes the "off the books" workers that earn a living but pay nothing into the system that rewards them because of their "rights" to have a place to live, food on their table and health care.

The privileged are the people who have the tax breaks and the savvy accounting techniques to lower their tax burden. These two categories are what push me to strongly desire a flat tax rate for all income, regardless of the level. If they make $100, they pay $10 in taxes. If they make $10 million, then they pay $1 million in taxes. No tricks and no games, pay the taxes on the income without having the right to reduce your taxes because you are wealthy enough to play with an accountant that can cook the books and funnel money into different areas to avoid taxation.

I also don't care who pays the tax. If an employer hires an illegal un-documented worker, as they do now, and they give them $100, then they had better send the $10 in for that income amount. Again, I don't care who pays.

The reason that this Depression is going to be the end of the middle class is because we are going to be hit the hardest and the longest. While the government is funneling all this money into the banks and the economy, they are allowing the executives at these banks to continue paying themselves outrageous salaries and ridiculous bonuses. Had these financial institutions not paid the brokers millions to continue writing more business, toxic business and potentially illegal business as we are finding out, then they would have had more money to keep on their books as reserves for their on-going operations.

We have now bailed out many of the banks. They are guaranteeing overnight lending between the banks. They have allowed all of these financial institutions to write-down huge amounts from their balance sheets to make them better so they can operate and be profitable again. These are write downs for bad debts and investments. They messed up, they got money from the government and they turn right around and start business as usual with diluted values in shares that are somehow in huge demand as their stock prices jump again when it is blatantly clear that the economy is still struggling, the consumer is still struggling, but they are working the DOW up all the time. How does that happen?

While these big banks and financial firms took their write downs and money from the government, they move forward without looking back. The middle class consumer is preyed upon by these credit card and consumer debt lenders through unscrupulous if not predatory methods. They get to deal with the collection agencies, which start collection efforts. If that does not work in a timely manner, and I don't see how it can based on the current depressed conditions in the economy, the collection agency will file a lawsuit against the consumer. If a client fell behind on a $30 per month payment because they are either unemployed, under-employed or just in over their heads due to the predatory credit lenders, how are they going to come up with a $250 payment to catch up with the past due payments and the late charges, or even the full amount should the account go to collection?

The collectors threaten to sue the clients for unsecured debt while the Wall Street firms have written off the debt already, and they are continuing to forgive secured debt. That makes no sense to me.

The problem is that after the initial lender has reported the account late for 30, 60 and 90 days, they then write it off and sell it at a fraction of the value. The account is then purchased at a much lower price and collection activities proceed for the full amount, even though most of the balance has been written off. The collection agency then hits the credit report with their derogatory line items. Bad credit is on for seven years. Legal items are on for ten.

So after the credit crisis is fixed and there is money to lend, who will be able to borrow it? It won't be the unemployed who will be receiving benefits from the government. It won't be the under-employed, which is all of the employees that had nice middle-management jobs with nice salaries for years that have had to take a position paying a fraction of what their salaries used to be. They won't be able to incur any more debt. Chances are they will barely be able to make ends meet already.

With the number of foreclosures and the amount of bad debt and the number of consumers with credit accounts in some area of delinquency or collections, will they be the target for the lenders? It's the same as when they target consumers who have gone through Bankruptcy based on the unethical theory that they are good borrowers because they can't file for bankruptcy again.

In the opinion of a credit lender, without the option of a Bankruptcy and with their ability to turn Unsecured Debt into Secured Debt, these are perfect clients. They will be even more likely to accept credit with terms that are not favorable, such as high rates and fees; substantial late fees and other penalties and possibly even a fee to borrow the funds. This is an absolutely wonderful position for the lenders.

Considering the fact that these consumers will now have access to new credit, it will be a perfect time to access the credit for fear that another financial crisis will occur and this way they will have credit they can fall back on in an emergency. But the emergency is often just living expenses and regular bills. The consumer will enter this cycle of relying on credit cards to improve their cash flow to pay other debts and the consumer debt problems will often repeat.

Because of the timeframe from when they will be extended the credit until the likelihood that things will have deteriorated to the point that they can no longer access credit to keep their heads above water, the initial lenders are taking their chances that their loans, at the high interest rates, will be paid back or paid off by that time and they will have made their profits and bonuses. Even if the account is never paid off, the consumer finding themselves back in this destructive position can take years and no one will question the lending decision made when a loan goes bad years down the road.

It was never a good lending decision based on ability to repay debt; it was a lending decision to be at the beginning of the relapse of the debt-relying consumer. Chances are the credit lenders will profit handsomely and that they also own or are part of a collection agency so that they can profit on the loans that do actually go bad.

Consumers need to be educated that they are being led down a dangerous path with consequences they do not even realize. While new regulations for credit lenders have been pushed so that the consumer is better protected, it's too late for many and unenforceable for others. Despite the fact that a payment is not recorded as late on credit until after it is thirty days past the due date, credit card companies have the right to increase the credit card interest rates from very low teaser rates to levels most people consider to be usury and they do it because they can.

7

Stock Splits

Stock splits are a calculated action with the sole purpose of deceiving the public. Let's assume a publicly traded company has one million outstanding shares. They can be owned by individuals, corporations, retirement plans and even by the company themselves.

Let's assume the stock is priced at $5.00 per share and it pays a five cent dividend quarterly for twenty cents a year. That's a four percent return. Also assume that this is the right price for this stock, based on the bottom line assets of the company.

The company wants to increase the value of the stock, and increase the assets available to the company, but the $5 price is as high as it should be. The company announces a stock split, giving two shares for each outstanding share. There are now two million shares of this company and the value of each has gone from $5 to $2.50.

Now to the professional trader, they know the real value of the diluted stock is $2.50 since the exact same company, with the exact same assets, has now tricked the consumer into thinking the stock is at a bargain price.

"This stock was at $5 just a few weeks ago. Numbers are strong with a year over year increase. The company has actually doubled it's holdings of its own company. That's a good sign." That's what the brokers may tell their clients.

Clients see this as a great opportunity to buy a stock that appears to be under-valued. But it's not. It's valued exactly where it was when it was a $5 but we've now been tricked into thinking it's a good deal.

Traders make the trades to buy the shares, getting paid on the transactions, the price of the stock stands a much better chance of going back up to $5 based on the movement and the client is happy because of the price increase and the company has now increased it's cash as their holdings of the stock have also increased in value.

Manipulation of the data is for the sole purpose of deception. Investors will call their stock broker and tell them to buy some of the stock of this company as they feel that they will be getting the stock at a bargain price. Even though they are getting twice as many shares for the same amount, based on the dilution of the stock by the doubling of outstanding shares, their investment in the company is exactly the same.

The senior managers and top executives, who are provided stock options and shares as part of their bonuses will benefit most from these stock splits. Their numerous shares will most likely rise in value, theoretically doubling in value back up to the initial stock price.

As a further example of the stock manipulation to deceive the public, when the price of a stock has dropped significantly and the public perception may be negative about the company, they will sometimes do a reverse stock split. Instead of the standard split where the numbers of shares owned are increased, the numbers of shares are diluted and reduced, thereby increasing the value of each share, to give the false impression that the price has increased. One thousand shares of a one dollar stock are worth one thousand dollars. If they do a ten for one reverse split, the stock price is increased to ten dollars and they now own one hundred shares. The value is still one thousand dollars. Unknowing investors will believe the stock price is increasing and will be more likely to invest in the company.

8

Flat Tax Rate

A Flat Tax would make life a lot easier for everyone. This includes the tax-payers who fear tax season. Trying to struggle their way through tax time is a major event, as evidenced by so many people putting it off until the deadline.

The wealthier the tax-payer, the more likely they have a highly compensated tax preparer that will find them every loop-hole so that they can keep more of what they make and legally lower their taxable income amount, thereby lowering their tax liability.

For the lower income families, they are at a lower tax rate already. The wonderful middle class, however, is once again screwed to the wall as they can not afford to have the highly educated tax preparers and they are taxed at progressively higher rates.

With a flat tax, let's say 10% of every dollar, it would make it very easy to calculate. The form would be one page long, with very few lines and would save billions of trees by eliminating multiple pages of forms. It would eliminate the need to review every tax return. Make it 10% for federal and 3% for state taxes. That's it, it's done. There are no deductions, no write offs, no refunds, no rebates.

The sales tax does not care what tax bracket you are in and that makes it a flat rate for everyone. If they really wanted to be fair, the sales tax paid when items are purchased should be different for every borrower. Why should a lower income tax-payer pay the same tax rate as a wealthy tax-payer?

The reason they should all pay the same is the same reason there should be a flat tax. Everyone will bring home a certain percentage of the money they earn. If they want to make more, they can earn more, not benefit from accounting practices. The ability to encourage workers to want to make more money, so they can have more money, save more money and spend more money is a wonderful concept.

The Alternative Minimum Tax, which was designed many years ago to tax the wealthy, now affects more people in the middle class than was ever anticipated. The wealthy are able to have their accountants find the laws that allow them to move money around and put it in places so their tax liability is lower.

In order to make the flat tax rate work, everyone needs to pay taxes on every dollar earned. This means that we have to stop turning a blind eye to cash laborers and under the table employers. Regardless of what you call it, there are income taxes not being paid into the system for those workers who work off the books.

The idea that the company is paying the tax for that worker since they don't have a way to write it off is ridiculous. They are not paying unemployment tax or social security taxes into the system. They don't have insurance so when they are sick or injured they get free medical treatment.

As for all the benefits that are being given to people, anyone, require that they be productive parts of society in order to get benefits. If they can work, they work. And if they can't work, make sure they can't work. If they can't do physical labor, find a desk job they can do.

We need to stop being a society of giving to people that don't deserve to receive it. They are called "illegal aliens" for a reason. It is because they are here illegally. The United States spends a lot of money, manpower and resources for border patrol, Immigration and Naturalization and national security. Someone entering the country illegally has broken the law. There are legal ways to come into the country and that should be the only acceptable way to get here, much less to get money, housing and health benefits.

The argument that they are taking jobs that American's don't want was never a valid argument, and especially now with the current environment of unemployed. It's adding to the problems we are experiencing.

On the same concept concerning foreign workers taking American jobs, during 2008 American finance companies applied for approximately 24,000 work visas for foreign workers to come to the country to work in the financial services industry. This was during the same period of time that the firms were laying off their own American workers.

The banks get taxpayer money to bail them out, they pay bonuses using that money, they use the money for things other than lending as it was intended, they lay off workers in the United States and not only do they out-source their call centers as much as they can, they are also applying to bring foreign workers in for jobs that should be filled with America workers.

What's most appalling about this is that these are all things that are not discussed. These are business decisions made by public companies with total disregard. Shareholders should be disgusted with business done in this manner and something should be done about it.

9

Shareholder Call to Action

American Shareholders can make a difference. We have seen it with Mutual Funds that concentrate on "Green Companies" or companies that are focused on babies and focused on any other specific areas that are important to the shareholders.

Shareholders need to be attentive and alert to the actions of companies they invest in. Countrywide was laying off employees and home owners were losing their homes to foreclosure while they planned an expensive ski trip vacation for their sales representatives and their best clients. This trip was cancelled due to the overwhelming negative feedback from the public.

Tuesday January 27, 2009, Citigroup cancels an order for a $50 million private jet for the company, supposedly after being pressured by the Obama Administration.

This is the same Citigroup that signed a twenty year agreement with the New York Mets for the naming of the new ballpark at a cost of $400 million. To make these decisions during this financial crisis is unbelievable especially when you consider that they anticipate twenty four thousand Citi workers could lose their jobs in 2009, and that does not include the workers laid off in 2008.

Citigroup has received $45 Billion in government aid, that's taxpayer money, and this is how their senior managers and Board of Directors feel is appropriate to spend money. Chances are Citigroup will not even be around in a few years. The Mets should upgrade all of their signs in the entire stadium so that they can be changed immediately by computer. That way, when Citigroup goes out of business and the bank is bought, the signs can all be changed.

Most of all, I feel bad for the Mets. They now have to have their franchise associated with Citigroup. That could have a terrible impact on the actions of their fans. Think of how many unemployed and struggling fans will snub spending one cent in that new stadium. They'll watch the games at home and even at a local restaurant, but as far as setting foot inside, never.

Shareholders need to be advised of major expenditures. I am not talking about responsible business operations which would include proprietary and private information concerning running the business, I am talking about the ancillary expenses such as paying for naming rights on a ball park. There can be an e-mail vote of all shareholders. They can be notified via e-mail and they would have 48 hours to voice their opinion and cast their vote for their shares.

If the shareholder does not respond within the specified time frame, their right to vote would be given to the Board of Directors to act as they see fit. A log for all votes would be needed to ensure that e-mails are not being sent to the wrong addresses or purposely not being sent to the shareholders.

To avoid a situation such as John Thain of Merrill Lynch spending $1.2 million to redecorate his office, it would be put to a vote of shareholders. Had that money not been spent on the project, it would have been profits that should have been distributed to the shareholders. When you combine multiple projects of $1.2 million for redecorating and $20 million per year for a ball park named after the company and throw in a few board meetings on the Hawaiian Islands with spouses for a week when you could have met with the same people in the conference room at the end of the hall, you start to see how the waste can add up.

Shareholders have a right to acknowledge how their money is being spent. If the executives want to spend $50 million on a private jet, it should be voted on by the shareholders. Have the company present their case. Have them outline the reasons that they need that private jet and how it will be used and the anticipated benefit to the company and the shareholders.

If it will be used in a manner that significantly improves the bottom line and productivity of the company, let's vote for them to have a private jet. If they plan on traveling to Washington, DC in that private jet to ask for government bailout money because they have driven the company into the ground, we may not be so inclined to approve that expense. A majority of their travel can be done on commercial flights. They may need to wait in a line or two and sit next to someone that they don't know, but they will get over it, since it is for the good of the company and the shareholder and that is why they are there, as an employee of the company, working for the shareholders.

If shareholders see that the company is not acting in their best interests, they can remove the money from the company and invest in another company that may be more in line with reality and how things should be done.

If the executives don't like the idea of having to answer to their shareholders and be accountable to them, maybe they should take the same steps as John Delorean and start their own company with their own money and do the things they way they want to do them. It's been a while but I don't think that worked out quite as well for John DeLorean as he would have liked it to.

10

Section 8 Housing

There are several things that really make no sense about section 8 Housing. Section 8 Housing is to provide housing to people that can't afford to live in homes that they want to live in. The program was introduced in 1937 as the U.S. Housing Act.

Based on information provided on the US Department of Housing and Urban Development website in February 2009, they indicate that they are not accepting any new applications but that they are continuing existing commitments. They note that as of September 30, 1996 (that's more than twelve years ago) there were four hundred thousand families being assisted.

The same website also disclosed that the cost of the program was $15.5 Billion in 1996 and $16.7 Billion in 1997. Why are the statistics so outdated on the HUD website? I find it hard to believe that they don't have more current statistics than from 1997. With four hundred thousand families being assisted in 1996 I guess we have to try to guess whether the numbers have gone down or if they have gone up.

The basic premise is that if someone wants to rent a home, and the cost of the home is $2,000 per month, but their income only qualifies them to pay $300 per month towards their rental, then the government pays the additional amount, $1,700 in this case, which gets paid directly to the landlord every month.

The program is based on very low income renters to have the ability to choose the housing of their choice, with a maximum of thirty percent of their income going to paying rent, and the Public

Housing Authority paying the difference, based on eighty to one hundred percent of the fair market rent.

Just based on this information so far, it is already a ridiculous premise. First, what justifies this person to live in a $2,000 home? They can rent an $800 apartment. In that situation even if the renter could only afford $200 per month, which would be thirty percent of their income of $667 per month for an annual salary of $8,000. The difference would be paid towards their rent until they can improve their position and pay the entire amount on their own.

But that is where it starts to get ugly. First, there is no time-frame for Section 8 housing. It goes on forever. The basic idea removes the ambition for people to do better, make more money, move up, etc. Instead of living in a $2,000 per month home on a $20,000 salary, if they made more money and lost their Section 8 Housing benefit, they would have to have a salary of $60,000 instead of $20,000 to be able to afford the same home.

From the $60,000 there would be additional taxes and the person would have to then pay the entire $2,000 a month. While I hope that all people move up and get better jobs, it is unlikely that the normal progression is from a $20,000 a year job to a $60,000 a year job, further stalling the consumer from ever wanting to or having the ability to make a change.

Making money on the books quite possibly has a negative result with their lives and cash flow. The recipients of this benefit will not look to improve their positions. They will work off the books, forever taking money for their rent while earning money they will never pay taxes on.

And if by some chance the government decided to spend money checking into the Section 8 Housing recipients and if they are making money off the books and if they have other people living with them, contributing to the household family income that may cause them not to qualify for Section 8, what do they do?

Public opinion may well be that they are picking on the lower income citizens. If they make $20,000, and they have $1,700 of their rent paid (times 1.2 to take into consideration the gross income needed to pay the rental amount=$2,040) and the fact that they may be working off the books earning cash and not paying taxes ($300 a week X 1.2 is $360).

Now they have a $20,000 gross salary, $24,480 in housing allowance and $18,728 in non-taxable under the table income. Their gross income is $63,208, which is a very nice salary.

Another problem with this is that the $1,700 per month for the rent paid by the government plus the $60 per week, $3,120, for the taxes not collected on the income, is paid for totally by the American tax-payers.

How many people are receiving Section 8 Housing right now? How long have many of them been receiving the benefit? It's absolutely out of control to pay for anyone's housing, potentially forever.

My suggestion for Section 8 Housing is that they all live equally. One family of 4 getting assistance living in a 2 bedroom apartment for $800 per month compared to another family of 4 who managed to get Section 8 Housing for a 4 bedroom single family home where they could potentially rent out the other two bedrooms and even have additional occupants living in the basement or attic apartment for $2,000 a month, is not fair.

The housing should be provided in projects intended to assist them move forward but not reward them for the situation. Apartment complexes would be the best, where all one bedroom apartments are the same, as are all of the two, three and four bedroom apartments. One family of four does not get 600 square feet while another family of four gets a 2,500 square foot home.

The units would be assigned based on the number of people. A family of four would get a two bedroom. A family of five would get a three bedroom. If they have another child while they are in Section 8 Housing, they would qualify for a move-up to a larger unit.

On-site services would provide child care so both parents could work. Career and job-placement services would be available in the community. ID's would be issued and checked to make sure the authorized recipients of the Section 8 Housing are the only ones staying in the units, unless they get approval for a short-term visit.

Section 8 Housing benefits should also have a time frame. The monthly payment made by the recipients will gradually increase over time. They could get 24 months of benefits based on initial criteria. For the third year the payment would increase to make their contribution greater, and increase slightly every six months to prepare the recipients to move to a private housing unit.

Section 8 Housing should work the same way as unemployment. Unemployment has a timeframe and a specific benefit. It also provides services to help get the consumer employed again to become a productive part of society instead of just having money given to them with no end to the benefit.

11

Forward Looking Markets

There is no doubt that the markets are forward looking. This is the explanation when the markets are moving in a direction that would be seen as contrary to the expected movement based on current economic data.

For instance, when the unemployment numbers were released in February of 2009, they were so bad that the market started to improve with the mentality that things had gotten so bad, that it had to be at the bottom and on the way back up. Now the number of times that they have predicted that the bottom was finally hit has been overwhelming. Calling the bottom of the market is just another way for the traders to justify their buying of stocks to increase their trades.

When the dust has settled and they realize that the economy can and will get worse, they become bears again and the bulls take a step back. For traders that get paid based on a transactional basis, bulls and bears fighting it out to support their theories and forecasts is a continued pay day for them all.

The forward looking part of the markets can best be summarized as traders "looking forward to their new vacation home or their new car". That is the true forward looking that the markets deal with. And for every trade, another slice of the equity in the financial markets is peeled back and paid to the traders and the managers to continue to do nothing but speculate and trade the stocks.

There are days that appear to be determined by the traders as they are entering the building. "Let's run it up 400 today" is probably a common statement with the "Take it down 400 today" being the next days mantra.

12

Unemployment Numbers

Have you ever thought about the unemployment numbers? The fact that ADP reports their numbers and makes the market move on their numbers is one thing. The fact that they normally don't line up with the government statistics is another.

They are a corporation with financial motivations for the economy to move in certain ways and the fact that they can provide "market influencing data" is ridiculous.

Even the numbers reported by the government are often skewed or even changed a month later to the "real numbers". Unemployment goes down around May of every year. That's when the college students come home from college and get part time jobs. That's not really an employed American.

The market also moves based on specific unemployment figures. It's hard to imagine that they are very specific as they are always rounded to the nearest thousand. The "estimates" from the "experts" suggest 345,000 new claims and it only comes in at 344,000 so the market must be getting better? That's a ridiculous way to reason that the market should improve.

But what did we miss about the 344,000 newly unemployed? That number is the most recent additions to the ranks of the unemployed. When unemployment benefits run out for a person, it does not mean they are now gainfully employed. The unemployment number only takes into consideration workers actually looking for work. Many actually stop looking.

Many people coming off unemployment are also now underemployed. That is terminology for the employee that took a job just for benefits and to try to keep their head above the financial water level. If they were a $150,000 middle manager and after ending unemployment they accepted a job at $75,000 a year, what do you think that does to the economy overall? Maybe it does not have an immediate impact, but over time it will cause more issues.

At $150,000, that person had cash flow to pay their bills, spend and perhaps even save some. Going out to dinner does not happen nearly as often with the reduced income. This will ultimately affect the restaurants, the retail stores and more.

The only sector of the employment numbers that increased with the most recent numbers was the one sector that we should not want to see. Government employment is up. As the largest employer, that makes the financial burden that much more on the consumers and for a much longer period of time.

There are a lot of the "not as bad as expected" movers in the market all the time. For example, a major financial institution wrote down $9 Billion dollars and needed to raise $5 Billion to stay in business. That may sound bad to normal people, but the "experts" had expected it to be a $9.1 Billion write-down and needing to raise $5.1 Billion. This makes it a tremendous success for the company since it was not as bad as expected.

Normal market movement for this stock would be up as it was not as bad as people thought it would be but what were they using to determine the estimates? What are people thinking? Of course, these numbers nearly put the company out of business so this "MUST" be the bottom of the entire financial crisis. Quick, everyone get on board because this justifies buying the stock so we don't miss it going back up to where it was before.

Analysts spend a lot of time going over the unemployment numbers, what the recent trends are, what the four week running average is, and trying to make heads or tails of how the unemployment percentages are affecting the economy.

There seems to be one thing that none of them bring up, and that is the under-employment of America. Many of the people being let go right now were professionals and managers, many from the financial services industry. Retail employees, pharmaceutical sales, builders; there is no escaping this tsunami of a financial crisis.

Many of the recently laid off were making substantially more than their unemployment benefits and more than the jobs they will be able to find when their unemployment runs out.

If a person was making $100,000 a year, there was a certain amount of cash flow going back into the economy. Even if there is another income in the home, it will probably have an impact on future spending.

As that amount decreases, it will affect the restaurants, the vacations and retail purchases. This decrease in discretionary income will ultimately have a negative impact on the economy. Discounts started over the summer for Christmas shopping. Knowing that there was a reduced amount of funds shoppers would be using, the stores battled for the customers to spend their money in their stores. Gift card sales dropped as consumers worried that the stores would not be in business when the gift was given.

Discounts were so big that it would be impossible for them to make a profit and probably even to not lose money. They did it for cash flow, to pay their bills and salaries to get by for as long as they could, hoping that things would get better before they really had financial troubles to deal with. Retail sales numbers may have not been as bad as expected, but earnings will be down drastically, even with the layoffs and the cost- cutting measures in place.

13

Credit Cards

Consumers should be limited to several credit cards at any given time, with credit card companies encouraged to compete for the clients. However, it should be illegal for credit card companies to clearly over-extend clients with credit without the basic understanding that if the consumer had more income, they would not be increasing their outstanding credit card balances every month.

Computer programs would be available to determine an amount of available credit for that client and that would be the amount of credit extended. Credit card companies should be accountable for the destruction of a consumer's credit report and scores. They are in the business of lending and lending is not giving credit to everyone that requests it.

The other idea is to have every credit card secured. I have a huge problem with the perception and the reality of what secured means and what unsecured means. If in fact a lender is providing unsecured debt, it should be just that, unsecured debt. The debt should not be convertible to a secured debt later when the consumer is having financial problems. Unsecured is unsecured and secured is secured. Do away with the ability of credit card companies to sell your account to a collection agency who then sues you for the full balance in search of a judgment, garnishment or some other court supported abomination.

How can the laws of the United States allow this illogical and mathematically impossible process of collection agencies being allowed to collect for the full amount of a debt that has gone bad and had a majority of the balance legally written off through accounting fundamentals. How well have the lobbyists done their jobs in getting so far inside the political anal cavities that they can dictate and control legislation to that level?

This is the type of legal and moral injustice being used to beat down and hold down the average American citizen so that they may never fully recover from the stress and pressures they will go through. The politicians accept funds from special interest groups to see things their way. The politicians need to be there to protect and serve the voters that put them into office and do the right things.

By limiting available credit it will curtail the careless spending which drives up consumer prices and hurts the economy overall with bankruptcies, collection accounts, charge offs, judgments, etc. Allow consumers the opportunity to apply for, receive, use and repay debt from an early age. But discretion and sound lending decisions should be used. College students need a credit card, but their credit lines should be several hundred dollars, not thousands of dollars.

For consumers that are self employed or in some other business where their tax returns may not show the true income of their work, a sound lending decision can be made by looking at their prior credit history, the money that have saved and what it is they actually do. If they have had issues paying, if they have no verifiable assets and they can not verify their income amount, the chances are that this may be an application to decline. Yes, decline, and for the credit lenders out there that don't know what that means, it is as simple as not giving credit to someone who probably can't afford to pay it back.

For the best clients, based on the actual review of the information, provide them with the best rates and terms. These rates should be slightly higher than mortgage or car loans because they are not secured, but not much higher because the underwriting criteria utilized to make the lending decision has determined that this is a relatively safe investment. Not secured in any way manner or form, just better than most.

The next levels would progressively have higher rates to correspond with the actual risk associated with every individual borrower. The lower the score, the higher the rate will be. If you are unable to verify income but everything else is good, then be ready to pay a little higher than the best consumers.

As you get closer to the bottom of the lending pool, where you have poor credit, can't verify your income and you have no assets, be ready to pay through the nose, pretty much the range of twenty to thirty percent that many cards charge now, for the honor of having a credit card.

The credit card can be secured with an asset account or semi-secured. For instance, if you give them $500 they will give you a $1,000 credit limit. If you have the assets to set aside to establish your own initial credit limit, do yourself a favor and get a pre-paid card from a local store and refill the card as you need to. There will be no monthly payments that can get lost in the mail, no late charges and no over-limit fees that you did not know about. It will allow you to avoid the headaches and pitfalls of a regular credit card company and make your life much simpler. You will also have the benefit of never having a collection call.

Visa and MasterCard are reporting huge profits. Do you think it is because they have provided credit cards to the right consumers? No, it's because they have provided credit cards to all consumers and many of them with multiple Visa's and multiple MasterCard's. How can these two monster companies not know that they are over-extending these clients? The problem is they do and they just don't care.

They collect transaction fees; cash advance fees, over-limit fees and late payment fees in addition to interest rates that meet usury levels by any sane person's evaluation and determination. Once again, this is clearly the power of special interest lobbying and politicians controlled by big business.

They provide credit to anyone and everyone. The cards are used, income is generated and when a borrower does go bad, they sell it for a percentage on the balance just to get it off their books, they take the legal write-downs so that their gross income is reduced and they pay less taxes, just as it should be correctly logged in a ledger book; the credit side and the debit side should match. They don't match and the consumers are the ones paying the price for this creative accounting being done on behalf of the collection agencies.

14

Car Insurance

Car insurance can be an expensive but required item. To drive a car you legally must have a valid driver's license and active insurance. Insurance is even more expensive for those of us to carry coverage, because we are also paying for un-insured motorist insurance.

That terminology has always confused me. Why do they recognize an "uninsured motorist"? There should be no such thing. It's the same as saying that there are different rules for "underage drivers". Obviously underage drivers are not permitted to drive.

When I first got out of college, I had a very close friend whose father owned an insurance company. I sent him a letter asking him the questions about why my insurance was so high and why I had to help cover uninsured drivers.

He had my letter printed in an insurance trade magazine along with his response. His response was that I was a conscientious member of society that took into consideration risk vs. reward. If I was in an accident without insurance or with insufficient insurance, I could very well be sued and lose much more than the cost of the insurance premiums.

He also educated me on the penalties of driving without insurance. He told me that if a person was found to be operating a vehicle without insurance, they were subject to a penalty and that they lost their license until they could provide evidence of insurance.

That seemed fair, as I assumed they would have to pay the insurance coverage amount for the period of time that they were driving without insurance. That was not the case.

If the driver had been driving a car for ten years without insurance, they would just need to go get insurance at that time in order to get their license back. There was no guarantee that they would pay the remaining premiums on the insurance they had just documented.

I feel that cars should be registered and if they are registered, they should have insurance on them. That means always. If a driver has a car and drives for five years without having insurance, if and when they are caught, they should have to pay the amount for the current insurance and also the full amount as calculated for the insurance amounts they should have paid into the system.

This would also help reduce the number of cars on the road to cars that are insured. If the car is pulled over for any reason, regardless of the driver, and there is no insurance, the state or town now owns that car. If the car has been stolen, the car thief goes to jail.

Set up a few EZ pass screens around the most heavily traveled roads. If the ones on the highways can recognize my car doing 65 mph and knew to charge my account number for that specific toll, there should certainly be an ability to recognize every car that is registered and insured.

If it is not registered or insured, have it pulled over.

A bar code on the top of every car, with a laser reading across a street will get every car, no matter how many lanes or how fast they are going. A little bit Big Brother like? I absolutely understand that. We are losing some of our freedoms but that is going to happen based on the technology. It needs to be our choice to use that technology to benefit society as a whole.

15

Extending Credit
is a Business Decision

Bank of America goes into business with other parties all the time. (Side note, Bank of America is currently still in business as of this time in February 2009 but based on recent information I would not be surprised if they were out of business by the time this goes to print) It can be in the form of investing in a stock or a fund to generate a profit. If that investment makes money, they make money. If that investment loses money, they lose money. That's business.

By sending out their offers to extend credit, often up to $50,000 or more, as a pre-approved line of credit, and they provide those funds to people just for signing their name and accepting their offer, they have gone into business with that person.

They are looking for that person to repay that debt so they can make a profit. And let's be serious, who is likely to accept a $50,000 offer of funds? It's the person that NEEDS the funds, not a person that doesn't. They know this.

And when a business struggles, the investment turns out to be a bad investment. Bank of America should have done more due diligence and used common sense to make a lending decision. There was no prior business relationship with them. They mailed out pre-approved marketing materials. They probably mailed out millions of them.

This ends up being a bad investment on their part. They will take a loss on this one. Some will go bad, that is the inherent risk with lending, as there is risk involved. Hopefully the majority will not have difficulty paying them and the overall performance will be profitable and make the marketing campaign of giving away unsecured money a success. If not, maybe they will learn and adopt more sound lending practices in the future.

Bank of America can write down the loss off of their books to offset the profit income from other accounts. That's how the accounting works and why many corporations do not pay any type of income tax themselves.

The person that borrowed the funds from Bank of America will ultimately pay the price in the long run. From the negative reporting on the credit report to the collection efforts and the ultimately higher cost for future credit. It sucks for everyone.

How then would it be considered fair that Bank of America is able to pursue collection efforts and legal action against an unsecured account they offered to the consumer without verifying how they would be paid back? How can they ultimately write off the loss and have a collection company be awarded the full amount for an item already written off on Bank of America's books AND at the same time severely impact the future borrowing of the consumer?

When a public corporation has troubles it writes down the loss and may be downgraded by analysts so that their cost to borrow goes up based on exactly what it is, risk. The losers in that situation are the investors that own stock in the company.

An individual can be seen in the same light as that company. They ran into trouble and their business partner, the lender, has taken a loss. The consumer's credit is damaged, causing future lenders to charge higher rates to them if they borrow. That seems fair, and sufficient. Stock values are consumers lending corporations money, why is it a different set of rules going the other way?

16

Collection Agencies

How big is the collection business? How profitable is it to lend money to borrowers without making sure they can afford it? How big is the business of collections that harass, insult and annoy consumers on their way to ruining their credit, impacting their health and possibly their mental well-being?

It's pretty damn big. Based on 2006 statistics provided by the U.S. Census Bureau concerning Collection Agencies in the United States, here is some information that may make you take note of how big of a business these bottom-feeding predators enjoy.

There were 4,455 collection firms with 5,085 established locations and 143,356 paid employees with an annual payroll of $4,516,286,000. That is four billion five hundred sixteen million two hundred and eighty six thousand dollars.

The salaries alone are more than $4.5 BILLION. That does not include the office payments and leases, utilities and other expenses of the companies. Forty-three percent of the collection agencies have four employees or less. In 1998 there were 88,882 paid employees and that number was increased to 143,356 in 2006. I can only imagine how many collectors there are during The Recession of 2008 and heading into what will most likely someday be known as the Depression of 2009.

I did not grow up with, go to school with or ever meet anyone that expressed a desire to be a credit collector. They do it because it allows them to benefit from the pain and suffering of others. They need to say and do whatever it takes to get the client to despise the calls so much that they are willing to pay something.

They call homes from eight in the morning until about nine at night, knowing all too well that they are calling people that are having tough times and the additional stress that comes with every phone call is devastating to the consumer. These bottom feeders are just doing their jobs. That is well understood. But they need to remember that the people on the other end of the phone line may very well have things going on in their lives that take a priority over a store credit card payment.

Comments such as "You have to have the money to make a payment" and "Skip your mortgage or insurance to make this payment this month" are normal comments. For the most part, these are untrained and often uneducated telemarketers paid hourly and earning commissions to repetitively call struggling consumers to harass and antagonize them enough to make payments. They don't care. Many of them have worse credit than the consumers they are harassing. They are not financial planners, financial consultants, or even financial advisors. They are telemarketers! If they do not have a level of understanding of the economy, there is no way they will understand that the people they are calling are collateral damage caused by the economy and the actions of many of their employers.

Many of the collection agencies are aggressively confrontational. They are abusive. There are collection laws in place to protect the consumer, FDCPA, the Fair Debt Collection Practices Act. The insults and degrading comments are a violation. Being abusive is a violation. An internet search for almost every collection agency will result in numerous complaints and pleas for help from consumers that are constantly being harassed illegally by third parties that are trying to collect an incorrect balance on an account that was never lent by them.

Changes need to be made. The number of collectors and collection agencies shows that this is a very large and profitable business. They produce nothing, they provide no service that benefits society and they are a detrimental part of society that causes pain and suffering, mental and physical, for the benefit and gain of no one except for themselves.

Debtors prisons were outlawed a long time ago and changes to the credit lending and collection practices in the United States need to step up and get with the times in an attempt to protect consumers.

17

Unsecured vs Secured

Unsecured Debt may be one of the most interesting phenomenon in the financial services industry. Lenders clearly do not correct consumers when they are under the impression that a credit card is an unsecured debt. They obviously did not secure any physical property with the credit, so it would be safe to assume that it is an unsecured product that carries the penalties of destroying their credit and making it difficult or more expensive to borrow money in the future.

We have all been wrong about credit cards being unsecured. If an unsecured credit card will ultimately be converted to a legal action and enforced by law, which is clearly a secured item.

Secure(d) means "free from risk or loss". The opposite would then also be true, that Unsecure(d) means "potential for loss". If lenders provide unsecured funds to a borrower they can potentially face a loss. If they face a loss, they should not be able to convert that account to a secured account and then collect the full amount.

Secure(d) also means "to give a pledge of payment to a creditor or to an obligation (a note by pledge of collateral)". Again, if unsecured, those pledges of payment to a creditor or an obligation do NOT exist.

Amazing, so what would "un-secured" be defined as? Unsecured is not in the Webster Dictionary of 1977, which means that it has become a main-stream term since then.

An on-line search found the following definition of unsecured debt:

- money supplied without supplying collateral
- a debt that is NOT guaranteed by collateral
- a debt that is not guaranteed by a piece of real or personal property. If the debtor defaults, the creditor does not have the right to seize specific property to satisfy the debt

Let's assume an original creditor loans $1,000 to a consumer at 25% interest without any type of due diligence except to look at their current credit report and credit scores. No income documents are provided to calculate the ability to repay the debt.

The $1,000 is used. They have the card for 5 years and with interest at 25% that is $250 per year, $1,250 over the five years. That is a total of $2,250. Five years of payments at $20 a month is $1,200. Balance after the five years remains around $1,000.

Something happens, a job loss or s negative situation, and the borrower can't afford to pay. They miss a payment and incur a $39 late charge. Now, to keep current, they have to pay the $20 missed, the $39 late charge and the next months payment of $25 for a total of $86. After two months they fall behind and they owe the original $20, two additional payments of $25 and two late fees of $39, for a total of $148. Late charges normally get paid first.

The collection calls have come from the creditor. They try to work with you to get your payment, possibly by an automated payment from your checking account, but things are just too tight and you can't do it. The account gets written off by the original creditor and goes to a collection agency. We will call them the predators. Your new balance is now around $1,200, $200 more than your credit limit and you made $1,200 in payments over the years.

They sell it to the collection agency for 25 cents on the dollar, but they were not willing to settle with you for 25 cents on a dollar. The best offers you received were for 50 to 80% of the balance. If you could not pay $20 two months ago, just where do they expect you to get the $900 from now?

The creditor sells your debt of $1,200 for $310. They write off the remaining $932 from their books.

How many times can that money be collected or charged to you? They wrote it off as a bad debt and destroyed your credit. They then sell it to a collector who places items on your credit and continues to hurt your credit history and score and then does its thing to strong-arm you into paying some how some way.

Based on this practice, it is my belief that in the name of Fair Lending, that the government should outlaw the terminology "unsecured". Let the consumer know what they are really getting into. Perhaps the term would be better if it was "Delay-Secured" or "Someday Secured" or "Unsecured but you have to pay some day anyway." You see where I am going with this.

Houses, cars, boats, even animals can be secured. Secure radios, televisions, even secure the products being purchased but that disclosure is going to have to be very clear so the consumer knows that they will have to give back the item should they not be able to pay.

I would have no problem buying things on credit with the item being secured. For a credit card with a larger limit, every item purchased with that card would be subject to forfeiture to the lender. They would do OK with the CD's and other items such as that. They may not be interested in taking back any of the remnants of the Burger King Meals or haircuts.

How does a fully secured , excuse me, "delay secured" account justify a "risk" up to an interest rate near 30% when a "secured" lien subject to a home foreclosure or auto repo at much lower rates work? With the foreclosure, the house could be gutted, destroyed and the car can be wrecked but the "secured" part of that loan is actually less secure than the "unsecured" credit cards.

18

Traders Getting Paid For Trades

Does anyone else see that the traders are spending all of their time moving the same pile of crap from one corner of the building to the other and then back again? Let me explain my thought. Traders do not earn a living based on doing well; they get paid based on just doing.

That means that they get paid for every transaction they make, and it does not matter whether it is a good transaction or a bad transaction. I truly believe that most market movement is done in a pendulum manner to earn the traders on Wall Street, the people who play with money all day, to continue making trades back and forth with no regard to the ramifications to other people and industries.

For example, look at the bond market for the past year. The yield on the 10 year treasury is used as a benchmark for 30 year fixed interest rates as a 10 year period is actually longer than most mortgage loans exist before they are paid off or refinanced. By pricing them off of 30 years, the rates would be much too high for the period of investment.

The 10 year treasury yield moved in huge chunks, back and forth, based on any single, albeit minute, bits of information and there have been swings back and forth that moved the yield to make mortgage rates move three to five times in a day.

I truly believe that the "mode of the day" is determined by the market movers, the traders that lead the pack. When they come in and have the mindset that the bond yield is too low, that inflation is a concern and the traders say things like "financials have hit a bottom and we can feel that since one of the largest investment banks just wrote off $8 Billion", they are moving the markets just to move the markets.

The bond gets hammered that day, the financials lead the Dow higher and the stock market goes up 200 points. Now the mortgage rates have jumped up at that time, possibly making current home buyers lock in at the currently higher rate for fear that the rates will continue to go up, or a potential home buyer sees the rates go up and they decide to stop looking for a home at this time. Both have negative impacts on the economy,

First, the buyer who gets a higher interest rate now has a higher monthly payment which means they have less disposable income to put back into the economy by buying other products.

Second, the potential buyer, who had been in the market, and could potentially purchase a home thereby stabilizing housing prices from their continued decline, decides to not buy a home, only prolonging the pricing pressure on housing based on limited buyers.

This hurts the economy even more because it may have stopped them from selling another home, which could lead to multiple home sales; they remove that mortgage transaction, the title company transaction, the attorney, the homeowner's insurance policy, the appraisal, the home inspection, etc. That does not even take into consideration the new couch, refrigerator, beds and other purchases that the housing market fuels with its transactions.

19

Collateral Damage

The collateral damage from the current depression hits a lot of people on a number of levels. One of the problems with the way the mortgage industry has changed is that the pendulum has swung too far from one side to the other.

Just a few years ago the only test you needed to pass to get a mortgage loan was the "mirror test". The mirror test is where they hold the mirror under your nose to see if you are breathing and if you are, they will find a way to get your home loan approved.

To make up for the years that they gave one hundred percent financing to borrowers that did not make enough money, that did not have good credit, that did not have any of their own money and even to those that did not have a verifiable source of income, they are making it difficult for the good borrowers with any type of situation outside the box of the new conservative underwriting criteria.

Underwriting has always been based on guidelines, in fact they teach you that when you get in the business. They are called guidelines because they are meant to lead the underwriter, not to hold them to make decisions that do not make sense. Underwriting was a common sense function, which is why not everyone could be an underwriter and why lenders should never let an originator be an underwriter to approve their own loans. Countrywide branch managers were responsible for production numbers and underwriting. How convenient, and yet the independent mortgage brokers get the blame for this mess.

When you think of the main items that caused the crisis; 1) The moronic programs with ridiculous guidelines; 2) The pricing that did not accurately reflect the relative risk of products; 3) The physical underwriting and actual ability to approve or deny a loan file and; 4) The actual funding of the loan with their money based on their programs, their pricing and their employees underwriting the file to determine if they wanted it or not. The funny thing about these four items is that mortgage brokers do not actually do any of them.

Many FHA mortgage lenders have recently raised the minimum middle credit score for their loans to 600 and some to even 620. Several years ago Fannie Mae and Freddie Mac were allowing "common sense" loans below a 580. The key is that they had to make sense. Credit scores are a good starting point, assuming that the credit information reflected is one hundred percent accurate, which it very often is not, and the rest of the file fills in the pieces.

What is good about the file? What makes this a good loan? Those were the questions underwriters asked themselves as they underwrote files. Then they started gong through a checklist without any consideration for the details. While a $15,000 monthly income for a stated income purchase of a $500,000 home with no down payment qualifies as a no income verification loan, the fact that they held a job that could never possibly make $15,000 a month seemed to slip through the cracks. Combine that with the borrower being a twenty one year old with no housing payment history, no savings at all and minimal credit profile and that loan should have been denied and that broker cut off by the lender. But we all know where the greed thing landed us.

A past client came to me for help recently, struggling with some cash flow issues in keeping up with revolving debt. He missed a couple of credit card payments and the credit scores for him and his wife both fell to the mid 500's. They are definitely an FHA loan, and the FHA allows borrowers with challenged credit and first time home buyers to finance almost 97 percent of the purchase price. That leaves very little margin of error if this first time home buyer realizes that the costs associated with the house are more than they thought or if they fell behind when they were provided unsecured debt to furnish the house. This is a loan that meets FHA guidelines and whereas the borrower met the guidelines, the potential for a loss if the mortgage can not be paid is present.

At the same time, my past client is not able to get the best pricing for the FHA program and many lenders are just declining to even entertain doing the loan. This loan carries very little risk. The small mortgage loan is under $100,000 on a home worth more than four times that amount so the loan to value is less than twenty five percent. The documented and verified income more then meet the program guidelines and the proceeds of the new mortgage will pay off a majority of the unsecured debt currently causing the problems.

The home is in a very stable Bergen County town that has maintained the values better than most others and even if they reduced the maximum loan to value based on a declining market, there is still plenty of equity in the home. This client has more than $300,000 in equity. What are the chances he will walk away from this mortgage? Even with the missed payments, there has never been one mortgage late. If they had to foreclose, it is a lenders dream to have that much equity to work with to cover late fees, attorney fees, interest, etc. The bottom line is this loan carries the risk only of being an inconvenience. As far as this loan actually ever losing the lender money, it's not remotely possible.

Many years ago I realized that making good lending decisions was not very hard. Instead of thinking about the company you worked for as this big rich corporate giant that owed you so it was alright to push things through the system, the key to lending is deciding if you would risk your own money for the borrowers if you had the capacity to lend your own money. Underwriters that had life experiences that they could associate with a borrower always worked. When a divorced underwriter got a credit explanation that the reasons for the bad credit was because of a divorce, that underwriter would understand the situation and take that explanation and try to piece together the rest of the file to make a sound lending decision. This is what true underwriting should be like. It's what it used to be.

20

General Thoughts

- The government wants the banks to start lending more to give consumers more credit so they can go and buy more things they can't afford in order to save the economy. Who would they like to do the borrowing, the consumers that are so far behind on their mortgages and other debts or the consumers that have become one of the masses of unemployed? Either way, there are significant flaws with their thinking.
- "This is the most profound economic emergency since the Great Depression". President Barack Obama on Monday February 9, 2009 at 8:08 pm in television address.
- "This is not your ordinary run of the mill recession". President Barack Obama, same speech, three minutes later at 8:11pm. Sounds like a reasonable assessment from a man who has realized what he has gotten himself into.
- While testifying in front of Congress on Wednesday February 11, 2009, the CEO's of the largest banks were ask to state their salaries for 2008 and 2009 and to indicate the amount of any bonus. All stated their salaries and in reading from the same script, all stated they had not been awarded or not accepted a bonus. The surprising thing is that none of them mentioned that they did not receive any commissions. They also did not mention that they did not receive any overtime pay. They clearly addressed the question concerning their salaries and their bonuses.

Had the question been worded correctly so as not to be a symbolic snow job of the American people, it would have asked them what other types of incentives and perks they did get or would be receiving. This would include little things like millions of stock options with various exercisable maturity dates and fully funded deferred compensation accounts. Do you honestly believe that they are working for $1 a year?

- With all of the time, effort and money to save the banks, one has to wonder if the banks are worth saving. The Federal Reserve and the government have done all they can to pump money into the banks, take banks to a point of near nationalization, invoke new rules and regulations and other criteria to make sure the American people get their money back plus the interest to make it a profitable short term investment. The key question is how do the banks intend to make the amounts of money they need to make to pay the big salaries and bonuses as well as the normal operating expenses of a company when two of their major functions are lending and asset management. They have crippled the American public to the point that anyone that needs to borrow and is willing to borrow no longer has the credit profile to afford the rates they want to charge or even the employment to qualify for a bank loan. This will again lead to the banks needing more money from the government.

- Merrill Lynch made the decision to pay their bonuses in December of 2008, just before announcing their monstrous losses and prior to having the shareholders vote on the merger with Bank of America. While definitely questionable in their timing if not outright theft of funds for the benefit of a few, they paid out bonuses of $3.6 Billion. If this amount had been divided between the 39,000 employees of Merrill Lynch, every single employee would have received a bonus of $91,000. Instead, twenty people were paid more than $8 million each; fifty-three were paid more than $5 million and the top four bonus recipients received $121,000 million between them. Analyzing all of the things that Merrill Lynch did wrong to it's shareholders, to the majority of the employees and the American financial system would require a book by itself, but it's not hard to see that the coordinated effort to steal massive amounts of money worked for the thieves that pulled off this caper.

- President Barack Obama has the opportunity to help the American people when they need it the most. He needs to change the fundamental process and procedures of borrowing and lending. Lenders have the right to lend and borrowers have the right to borrow. Lenders can base the interest rate and terms based on their risk assessment of the transaction. They can't just give money to anyone and hope that they pay it back. It's a risk based transaction and needs to be entered into by all parties in that manner. If the lender feels collateral for the loan should be made, such as for a mortgage or car loan, they provide a financial instrument that includes a secured lien in the item. If they want to allow the consumer to buy a stereo or a television, they can also secure that property. If the consumer fails to make the payments for any reason, the lender gets to report them as a poor borrower to the credit bureaus, repossess the secured items and write down the actual loss when the secured instrument is sold. However, the rules are also the same for unsecured debt. If they provide unsecured financing to the consumer, it may carry a higher interest rate because of the actual risk, as compared to the implied risk based on the current rules and laws. If the consumer fails to pay, they report them as a poor borrower, they impact the credit score and they write off the loss as a bad debt at that time. Future lenders will either not lend to that borrower or they will charge a higher interest rate to offset the risk or even make sure they only lend them money that is secured so that have some collateral. However, the current rules where the lender writes off the loss and then the full amount of the debt still being due to a third party collection agency needs to stop. These unsecured accounts end up ruining the credit of the consumer, they get harassed by collection calls, they end up paying more for future credit, if they can even get it, they end up having legal items reported on their credit and then they are sued and forced to pay money they could not afford to pay in the first place. President Barack Obama was elected on a platform of CHANGE and this would be the change that would benefit the American people.

- The American people need to learn the difference between a Non-Profit Agency such as the American Red Cross and a Not-For-Profit organization, such as a privately owned consumer credit counseling firm. Non-Profits are more normally labeled as charities. They are raising money to benefit others and while the percentage of the money they provide to the actual beneficiaries varies by organization, based on their operating expenses, they do provide the funds to the needy. However, a Not-For-Profit organization is often a company walking a fine line. The owner of the company can claim to be a not-for-profit as long as the bottom line of the company does not show any profits. If the company makes a million dollars, as long as the owner of the company takes a full distribution of the income and the company does not show a profit at the end of the year, they are a not-for-profit. They are not the same. There should be better disclosure to the public and these organizations should have salary and overall compensation limits.

- Charities that solicit money from the public should not be allowed to sell your personal information to other charities. We all get so many solicitations asking for money we may not recall when they started coming in such mass numbers. Chances are that it was one of your heart-warming donations to a charity that caused you to get put onto a mass marketing list for every charity you can think of and probably many you never even heard of. Some charities accept your donation and then sell your name as a person that gives to charity so they can make more money while violating your privacy and giving your personal information to others. Choose the charities you want to give money to and make sure to check them out to determine what percentage of every dollar actually goes to the needy.

- While there are text book definitions that define recessions and depressions, the real world comparison is determined simply: When your neighbor loses his job it's a recession; when you lose your job, it's a depression. It does not get much simpler.

- Mortgage lenders are required to get a credit report for every mortgage applicant. They pay the credit reporting agency a fee for this information. The credit agency is then aware that the borrower is very likely looking for a mortgage loan because they are able to determine the type of lender that ran the report. The credit agencies then sell the name and information for that potential mortgage client to other mortgage companies willing to pay for the leads. This should be a violation of personal privacy of the consumer as their desire to secure mortgage financing is a private and personal transaction and advising third parties of this is a violation. It is also a horrible business practice to charge a client for a service, which is the charge to get the credit report, while at the same time undermining their relationship with the clients by providing that data to other companies.

- When is a write off not a write off? When a lender makes a bad lending decision they write off the loss on their books and the books balance, right? No, they write off the loss and the collection agencies are permitted to continue collection efforts on a balance that no longer exists based on basic every day math or any legitimate accounting practice.

- Does your bank still put a deposited check on hold when you deposit it? They may allow a small amount or a percentage to be available in the first few days, but they will often put a hold on the difference so they do not credit your account for a number of days, which means they don't have to pay you interest or give credit for the actual balance. This is an antiquated process that was required because banks had to physically deliver the checks to the clearing houses located throughout the country so that they could verify the funds were in the account before they credited and debited the accounts from each bank. This was a responsible way to limit losses and verify that checks were good, but it's not really applicable to the way the world works now. Transactions are instantaneous. Someone needs to tell the fat cats in these banks that there are things called the internet and computers they can use to speed things up. It's just another outdated loophole that allows the banks to take advantage of the consumer.

- The terminology "Ability to Repay" is the measure of the borrower's ability to meet current and future debt obligations. Consumers may have more than several active trade-lines, some of them opened recently and with balances. The available credit limits have been utilized and the consumer has credit inquiries on their reports that they appear to be looking for additional credit. Perhaps an underwriter should consider the fact that the ability to repay is becoming questionable. Yes, they have been able to pay and they have a good credit score. They have not missed any payments, but if they have sufficient income, why is the level of their outstanding debt rising. What training do the underwriters go through to make these lending decisions? Most don't even require any verification of income, just the credit score. Please pass this information on to the executives at the banks that put millions in their pockets while burdening American consumers with credit they should not have been granted in the first place.

- In the mid 1990's, there was a branch manager for the largest bank in New Jersey. This manager was always getting the awards for new accounts, the most personal loans and the most commercial loans. She was the manager that everyone was compared to and no one could even come close. After being with the bank for many years, a first year auditor, fresh out of college, was doing a random audit of the loans booked in that branch. In reviewing the files, this auditor felt that some of the signatures started looking similar. Turns out that this branch manager was writing loans for people that were not requesting credit. She would do a $100,000 loan for a person, take the money and use the proceeds of the loan to make the payments on that loan as well as the previous loans. She had several homes, nice cars and was always able to take nice vacations. But the loans that were booked by her were all bogus. This was a ponzi scheme. Unlike Bernard Madoff, the scheme did not come to a crashing halt because no more investors were available, this could have gone on forever, or at least until the minimum payments were no longer made. This was a random act of actually doing their job by a first year auditor. This auditor obviously never went to work for the FDIC of the SBLIC or any other agency responsible for catching these types of inaccuracies. The branch manager was never charged because senior management felt that if word got out that the bank allowed this to go on, that the investors might lose their confidence and trust in the bank and sell their stock or pull their money out of the branches. They let a felon go free to save their reputation and stock price.

- On September 10, 2008 Lehman Brothers (remember them?) was "De-Risking". They had a third quarter loss of $39.9 Billon, which was equivalent to $5.92 per share. At that time the shares were trading under $9.00. On Sunday September 14, 2008 Lehmann Brothers went bankrupt and Merrill Lynch worked out a deal to become part of Bank of America. The government showed that despite the "too large to fail" attitude, they had the ability to pick and choose who was going to survive and who was not.

- Debtor prisons were present in the United States until 1833 when President Andrew Jackson changed the rules. With the current rules in place for unsecured debt to become a legal item for full collection by a collection agency or a collection attorney even after a majority of the amount is legally written off by the lender that actually lent you money…it sure seems like a debtors prison to me, just without the bars.

- Mortgage brokers are blamed for the mortgage meltdown, the sub-prime crisis and anything else that has gone wrong with the world's financial system. Obviously there are bad mortgage brokers, same as there are bad people in every profession. Mortgage brokers provide services to mortgage clients that many banks don't and/or can't provide. When you call some big banks, you get a "Mortgage Specialist" who reads from a script, gives you basic information and then asks for your credit card to start the process. They offer their products and their pricing and that's normally it. A mortgage broker is most likely a member of the local community or at least from the same geographic area. Some brokers do operate in multiple states but it is the local mortgage brokers that will meet with you in person so you know who you are dealing with and very often the person you see on the ball fields in your home town. Mortgage brokers have the capacity to send your loan to a number of investors, depending on which lender best serves your needs. Not every lender offers every product. Not every lender is as aggressive every day. When a bank gets busy, they raise their rates to slow down business. If you happen to have that timing, your rate will be higher. A mortgage broker will research a number of investors and choose the best one. Mortgage brokers do not determine program guidelines. They do not set pricing. They also do not underwrite. A mortgage broker will prepare a loan file and submit it to a lender for review and a disposition. If the file meets their guidelines and they want the loan, they approve it. They also have the capacity to deny a file if it is not what they want. For some banks and lenders on Wall Street to blame mortgage brokers for the financial problems we are having is absolutely ridiculous.

- Imagine you are a life insurance salesman for a large company. The company rolls out a product for you to sell and it is a million dollar policy. It costs less than a hundred dollars a year to the client and there are no age restrictions or health requirements for the policy. The company was also going to pay you a five thousand dollar commission for every policy you sold. Could you sell that product? You absolutely could! There would be tons of people lining up to buy that policy from you and you would be seeking anyone you could to sell them this product, which you did not develop or price or approve. Who is to blame when the ninety nine year old clients you sold the policies to start to pass away? This is the same thing that happened when the greedy bankers put out products with pricing and underwriting criteria that made no sense at all. It's not the mortgage brokers fault; they sold the products provided to them at the pricing offered.

- A small Alternative-A Wholesale Lender in Northern New Jersey was originating the mortgage product line that ended up impacting the markets. They were providing loans up to one hundred percent financing. That's no money down at all, for borrowers with minimal credit histories, mediocre credit scores, no housing history and without verifying income and assets and sometimes not even verifying if the borrower had a source of income. If this sounds crazy to you, it was. But the company had investors on Wall Street paying them ridiculous amounts of money on rates not much higher than the Fannie Mae and Freddie Mac rates, but without the underwriting guidelines and restrictions. These are known as TPO's which stands for third-party originations. A mortgage brokerage firm would solicit the clients and prepare the file, they would send it to a wholesale lender for underwriting and if approved they would close the loan with the wholesaler and get paid for the loan. The wholesaler would then package up these loans into larger pools, so that they would make more money on them as a large group of loans instead of on a loan by loan basis and the Wall Street firms would bid on them and they would be sold to the highest bidder. Loans were supposedly underwritten, making sure that the loans met the guidelines and that there was no fraud in the file. Any loan includes risk, but when you are not looking at the documentation to verify information about the clients, there is often not much to go by. There were times when the employment information in a file was incorrectly stated, if not outright fraud, and hoping no one would check. Instead of denying the file, they would restructure it and close it anyway, knowing full well that loan was going to be a problem. But the liability that went with that loan was acceptable based on the amount of money they were making. More loans, more loans, more loans!!! The greed was at every level.

- Since American tax-payers are providing the banks with extraordinary financial assistance and support to get through the current economic problems, let's utilize this opportunity to do some house-cleaning. Transparency and disclosure are some of the hot topics based on the smoke and mirrors in the financial services industry. Let's have the assets for the company actually be an asset. Instead of taking a hundred million dollars worth of loans and splicing and dicing them to the point that they have been cross collateralized and securitized in more ways than is imaginable and listed on the books in such a convoluted manner that it's impossible to determine how they have come up with their numbers, let's make it simple. We'll start with the basics. An Asset is an Asset and a Liability is a Liability. I understand that a $100,000 loan on a home at 5% interest is a secured $100,000 asset, and I also understand that the potential accrued interest on that loan, which would be $93,255 is also an asset as the potential earned interest. But the reality is that most mortgage loans do not stay on the books for the term of the loan. If they list that loan as an asset at $193,255, there is very little chance that this will actually be accurate. Instead of an arbitrary percentage or time frame for that loan to exist, it could be broken down into five year pieces, with the earlier periods worth more because the higher principle balance will accrue more interest in that period than later periods. The first five year period would have interest calculated at $32,209. This would make the value of that asset $132,309 for the initial period and would be re-calculated based on current principle balance and whether or not the loan was still on the books for later valuation.

- The United States Government was never intended to be the largest employer in the country. At a time when every other industry is laying off employees and the unemployment numbers are sky-rocketing, the government is hiring even more employees to handle anything from the additional unemployment compensation requirements to the management of the money being provided through government funding. While the government provides funding to banks and other industries as well as the American people, they are hiring many more workers that will get their pay and benefits. History has shown, with very few exceptions, that a government job does not get eliminated. These are costs and expenses we can expect to carry for many years down the road. In addition to the expected increases in taxes to try to pay the interest on the trillions of dollars being given away by the government, we will now have to carry these additional salaries and benefits for the employees.

- The big business of charities soliciting money becomes insulting when they continue to mail you requests for money on a regular basis, with free mailing labels or a nickel or whatever their marketing methods may be, and they indicate that your donation is "PAST DUE".

- Nancy Pelosi pushed hard for the initial Economic Stimulus Package noting it was needed and imperative that we get it done to save the economy for the American people. They needed to send $600 to every person to give them the money that was needed for them to feel good about themselves, as if $600 changes anything for most people, and they pushed hard for it to pass. Soon after it passed, and before the checks could even be printed and mailed, it was Nancy Pelosi saying that the government was not doing enough and that more needed to be done. How quickly did she think the government would be able to generate and mail the checks? Also, this was a one time shot to put money into the hands of consumers and a hard cost to the government and the American tax-payer. A better option would have been to lower mortgage rates to the point that rates were attractive enough that home-owners could refinance their homes, remove those loans from the label of toxic, improve their monthly cash flow, which could then be used to put back into the economy, and the total number of toxic loans that the government might have to buy or bail out would be greatly reduced.

- Mortgage products should be risk based lending instruments. Fannie Mae and Freddie Mac should offer market rates for the best borrowers that can show their income and assets. There is no guarantee moving forward that the borrower will not run into financial difficulty, such as becoming ill or losing their job. The lending decision has to be based on the most current of information as a snapshot to determine eligibility. The credit bureaus negatively affect a lot of borrowers because the information on a credit report is often wrong. The same account may be showing more than once or an account that does not belong to the borrower. Even though I have difficulty with the credit scores and reporting procedures, I am not opposed to pricing adjustments based on specific credit scores and loan to value ratios. It will help determine overall risk on a file. Self-employed borrowers often do not claim as much on their tax returns because of accounting benefits. These are the clients that utilized the no income verification and stated income loans. They may be excellent borrowers with sufficient income, excellent credit and strong assets. However, because of their income method, they may not meet conforming underwriting requirements. Make risk based adjustments to these loans. Make the interest rate one percent higher with twenty percent down and two percent higher with ten percent down. The support for stated income loans is that the self-employed borrowers get a benefit by being able to reduce their tax burden, but they should not also get the benefit of the lowest interest rates. It's only fair that they get one or the other, but not both.
- Tip Jars at places like Dunkin Donuts? You have to be kidding me. Pour me a cup of coffee and put a donut in a bag and you want a tip? The entire transaction normally takes less than thirty seconds and that does appear to

be their jobs. Dunkin Donuts as a company should be embarrassed to allow this and to be associated with this. Do I need to tip the dry cleaner for getting me my clothes? How about the gas station attendant? Maybe the clerk at the supermarket would like a little extra. I don't see them asking for tips. When a waiter or waitress spends an hour serving us and taking care of us so we have a pleasant evening, tipping is normal and expected. Expecting a tip for putting a donut in a bag, that's just horrible.

- "Our capital structure was never designed to withstand this knd of pummeling from the outside world." Quote from Linens & Things CEO in April 2008. On May 2, 2008 they filed for Bankruptcy.

- On Friday April 18, 2008, Citigroup, the largest US Bank, posted a $5.1 Billion loss. This was the second straight quarterly loss, as they were hurt by $15 Billion in write downs and increased reserves for credit losses. Despite the loss, their shares rose $1.43 or six percent in pre-market trading. The bank had slashed its dividend and raised more than $30 Billion in new capital. They had $6 billion in write-downs and credit costs tied to sub-prime mortgages. They also had $3.1 billion in write-downs for loans to fund corporate buyouts. They even had a $3.1 billion increase in credit costs related to consumer lending and they also wrote down $1.5 billion of exposure to bond insurers and $1.5 billion for auction rate securities. "Results reflect the continuation of the unprecedented market and credit environment and it's impact on our historical risk positions." Chief Executive Vikram Pandit. So they get to write everything down to improve their financial positioning but the same items being written down are then sold to collection agencies for a fraction of the initial value and they get to collect for the full value? The consumer is getting screwed coming and going with this system.

- May 2008: There are 8.5 million unemployed and the unemployment rate is 5.50% compared to 5.0% in April. Unemployment numbers jumped by 861,000, the biggest one month jump since 1986. The government added 17,000 jobs. At a salary of $30,000 a year, these 17,000 new government jobs are an additional annual expense of $510 million, not including benefits, training, workstations and other applicable expenses. Consumer confidence hit a 28 year low.

- Tuesday July 22, 2008, Wachovia announces an $8.86 billion loss and slashes it's dividend. They announce 6,350 job cuts as their losses tied to mortgages soared. The losses did not soar, the mark to market losses overwhelmed them as the mortgage loans they had on their books, with a vast majority of them paying their mortgage on time, could not be sold to other mortgage investors in bulk because the secondary market had dried up. Despite most of the loans paying on time, the fact that they could not get top dollar for the sale of the pools of loans made them worth much less. Mark to market accounting had a major impact on this entire depression. If someone is willing to pay me five dollars for a ten dollar bill, what is the value of the ten dollar bill? If I choose not to sell it for the five dollars, what is it then worth? At the same time, going back several years when everyone assumed home prices were going to continue to climb, if a home was valued at $100,000 and they paid $120,000 for it, what was the value? These are the games the banks have been playing with their books, all to the detriment of the American people and the financial system. These results of the Wachovia write-down included a $4.2 billion increase for bad loan reserves and a $6.1 billion write off of goodwill. Goodwill? What were the accountants at Wachovia smoking to think they even had that amount of goodwill? How can they be allowed to have an "asset" such as goodwill on their books to throw off and deceive the investors and the public? After that $6.1 billion goodwill write off, just how much more of the assets on their books were considered goodwill? What's next, a $12 billion write down for a banks "Sense of Humor"?

- Thursday July 31, 2008, some of the headlines: "GDP (Gross Domestic Product) likely to show a gain mostly due to stimulus" taken from the CNBC home page. "The US economy probably grew modestly in the second quarter, but analysts believe Thursday's GDP report will mainly reflect the help of stimulus checks." Was an Economics degree from Harvard required to know this? No kidding! Jim Cramer of CNBC also indicated that the market had bottomed. Cramer once again moved the markets based on his own belief and his entertaining television show and clearly shows that his personal interests to entertain and be viewed are well above his interest to provide valid financial data.

- Many mortgage servicing companies are sending an appraiser to homes as soon as a payment is more than thirty days late. There are millions in foreclosure and many more borrowers that are thirty days, sixty days and even a number of months late on their mortgage that they are aware of, but they want to know what equity may be in your home so they know whether to sweep it aside for now and let it try to work or if they should proceed with any legal foreclosure process they can. For the homebuyers that never should have gotten the home they are in, the ones that did not put any money down, the ones that did not make enough to purchase the home in the first place, they are getting a benefit others won't get. Since there is no equity and the values have dropped, they are already in a negative equity position and the lender has nothing to gain by foreclosing. If nothing else, they are overlooking the problem to deal with it at another time. For the owner that has been in their home for years, paid their mortgage regularly and built equity in the property not only through appreciation but also through principle reduction, if they hit a tough time and lose their jobs and fall behind, the banks will work hard to foreclose on them. There is money to be had there, there is equity, and those are the homes they concentrate their efforts on. These are the owners that have earned the right to save their home, to be helped in any way possible. Once again, if you did things the right way, it all comes back to bite you.

- Fannie Mae (FNMA) CEO Donald Mudd had 2007 compensation of $11.6 million, including stock, salary and other compensation. Freddie Mac (FHLMC) CEO Richard Syron earned $18.3 million in 2007, as well as other benefits that included a car and driver, a home security system, travel costs for his wife and $100,000 to pay his lawyer to renegotiate his contract with FHLMC. Wow, all that and it was working for a GSE, a Government Sponsored Entity, which makes it almost a government job. How come I never see these positions advertised? Many other potential CEO's could have run these companies into the ground for much less compensation.

- Who owns the credit collection companies and why has the government taken a stance to protect them and back them in their illegal collection activities? Despite never having borrowed any money from them, they have the capacity to file a lawsuit to collect the entire amount of the original debt, despite the legal write-down of the balance by the creditor that actually lent the money in the first place.

21

Closing Remarks

After twenty-one years in banking and mortgage lending, I was finally able to squeeze in something to justify my five years of college with a BA in English: Writing Concentration. Don't be too critical of the grammar or technical issues with my writing. After many years of working with mortgage payments and trying to explain the mortgage process to my clients, I've tended to simplify and minimize the way I do things. I am sure that will show with the number of simple, basic sentences. Judge me if you will, but I am OK with that.

If you are reading this, there is a good chance you know me personally. You may have even listened to my ramblings about some of these topics. This has been very therapeutic for me, being able to get some of these feelings and thoughts out of my head and onto paper to help eliminate the disappointment, confusion and anger I feel about how things have played out.

When times are good, we tend to look the other way about things that may not be right. The tax system would be an example and so would the ridiculous salaries, bonuses and stock options paid to the top executives at companies where they have obviously forgotten that the shareholders own the company.

It can also be seen with the stock market. There were always swings in the market, up one day and down the next, all for the ultimate purpose of lining the pockets of the stock traders. While it appeared orchestrated all along, at the end of the day, after they took their billions upon billions to justify the bonuses from slicing off a piece of every transaction, when you got your statement at the end of the month and your balance was a little higher than it was last month, everything was still OK.

Now when the statements are received they are not even opened. People don't even want to open them any more because they have lost so much money. This is not play money like the government has, where they can just continue to print more and more to pay the interest on the deficit balance while increasing the deficit to the multi-trillion level. This is real money we have earned and saved that is just gone and many of us will never be able to recover that money in our lifetime.

Companies expanded and increased their sales every year mainly by selling to consumers who were using the equity in their homes and credit to make the purchases. That availability of credit is gone and I can't imagine when the American consumer will be ready to set themselves up for this type of pain again. They continue to say we need to get lending going again to get the economy back moving towards growth. Who is left to borrow? People with money don't want to borrow because they have the money and there is no reason to borrow. Even the very wealthy have been impacted by this depression and that has changed the way they are spending.

The credit card companies and the banks have selectively targeted consumers to extend credit to with no reasonable determination that they would be able to pay off the debt in good times, much less when the economy finds itself in this type of depression. With two million foreclosures and millions of people on unemployment and an estimated fifteen percent level for underemployment, who is going to be left to borrow? And if there is no borrowing, there is no discretionary cash flow for the purchases to support the retail stores and companies that will continue to find themselves with tighter profit margins and then laying off more employees and closing more locations. This is a vicious cycle that will continue.

Who will the banks lend to? Remove the unemployed, remove the poor borrowers that have lost their homes and remove the countless number of people that are fighting their way out of the debt they had piled on before. This tragedy was a carefully orchestrated effort by the foreign owned Federal Reserve Bank that went a bit too far and now they find themselves trying to repair it so that in five years they can capitalize on another credit bubble, housing bubble or technology bubble.

The banks rely a good deal on lending for their income. What numbers are they looking at to even think a recovery will happen? The idea that banks are making lending more difficult is an argument for later, but if making good lending decisions is part of the reason, that's understandable. We don't want them flooding the markets with extra money to consumers that can't afford it. The purchases they make with that money is not fair to the consumer when they can't make the payments as they should have never been given the credit in the first place.

My guess at this point is that banks will become nationalized in the not too distant future. It could happen before their third quarter of 2009. I believe they will become a quasi-government or GSE (Government Sponsored Entity) just as Fannie Mae and Freddie Mac are. This will help regulate the entire banking system. They can hire executives at realistic salaries that are accountable to the shareholders of the organization to provide them with a return on their investment instead of concentrating on their personal income.

Over the last fifteen years, if you remove the bubbles of equity and debt, there is no way the economy would have grown the way it did. Companies would not have sold the amount of products, made the perceived profits and watched their stock values rise as they did. These numbers and all the corresponding statistics are wrong. Now that we get back to reality, with the real income of the American workers relatively comparable to where it was fifteen years ago, and the equity and credit gone, how are these companies going to generate sales and profits? Many will be forced to lower their prices to compete with WalMart and this will shrink their profit margins, causing additional cut-backs and lay-offs.

$75 Billion has been earmarked to stem foreclosures. This money will be used to subsidize the housing payments for borrowers in risk of default. The government should have done more with the treasuries and Fannie Mae and Freddie Mac to lower mortgage rates earlier in the depression. Had they done that many of the good borrowers would have been able to refinance to a lower interest rate, improve their cash flow for discretionary spending to help the economy and remove loans originated in what is considered a toxic period and make them part of a "New And Improved" loan originated after underwriting started using common sense with their lending decisions. With the new rules and guidelines, these loans, at least at this point while they still have jobs, are excellent secured mortgage loans, and would no longer be lumped in with the toxic loans. Last reports showed that 93% of mortgage loans are still paying on time with no problems. All of this crap has to do with seven percent of the loans.

There is no way of telling what is going to happen next. It took the government twelve months to recognize that we were in a recession. I've referred to this as a recession because that's already been acknowledged. I have also referred to this mess as a depression; we may just need to give the government a few years to admit it. If they acknowledge it too soon it will cause additional panic and that's the last thing they need.

They are saving the banks, the insurance giants, the automobile industry, the homeowners that bought homes they could not afford and throwing money in all sorts of directions in hopes something will help. The issue that the government should be working on is correcting the credit lending and collection agency impact on the consumers. Make collection agencies and collection activities illegal. Throw the owners, managers and employees of the firms a few hundred billion and send them on their way. Let lenders make good lending decisions to borrowers that are going to be able to pay them back or don't lend the money. If the loan goes bad, write it off and report it to the credit bureaus for other potential lenders to see to determine the risk associated with that borrower. Without this reform the number of borrowers who will be able to borrow in the future will be severely limited.

Make lending a risk based process as it was originally presented and sold to the public. Make the rates lowest for secured loans where the collateral can be taken back. Increase the rates for unsecured loans and even increase the rate to relate to the risk when higher amounts are being borrowed. If a credit card for $500 charges 15% for the risk of that unsecured line, then make the $50,000 unsecured loan 20%. But remember, if that debt can't be repaid, the borrower and lender share the risk in that the borrower will now have bad credit and the lender will have lost their money.

Otherwise, with everything going on, my next book may be printed by the US Socialist Government Printing Society. Yes, Socialism is a real concern, regardless of what they call it or label it. After all, with the Federal Reserve we thought we were living in a free market capitalistic society with our own economy. We have been very wrong for a long time and if President Obama can deliver on his promise for CHANGE, these are things that need to change.

Thank You

Thanks to my wife Kathryn who is my "everything" and my sons Patrick III and James. These are extra-ordinary times and I am blessed to have an extra-ordinary family I love with all my heart.

Thanks to my Mom and Joe for doing all you could for me through the years. Thanks to my friends from Randolph, William Paterson College, Wayne Hills High School, the Passaic Optimist Club, Camp Ocawasin and the Passaic Boys Club...all of you have had an impressionable impact on my life.

Thanks to the Randolph East NJ Little League State Champions of 2007. It was a pleasure watching your hard work, your friendships and the ultimate achievement of your goal. To the parents of these fine players, we have spent more time together than most married couples and I look forward to having some Miller Lites with you for many years to come.

The Editor

David Gordon has a BA in English Literature and Political Science from William Paterson University. Gordon spent a year as an exchange student at Kingston Polytechnic and London School of Economics where he met and studied under Iris Murdoch and Benazir Bhutto. Gordon is currently a Sales Director for a US based technology company

NOTE: David Gordon is a friend and a Delta Psi Omega Fraternity Brother. I don't believe David knew what he was getting himself into when he offered to edit this for me. I explained that my ideas were conceptual and often written in one thought stream. As the editor, it's his job to do the real work. I have no doubt he'll think twice before making that offer again.

Contact Me

You can contact me with your thoughts and opinions at the address below. I am open to your feedback, criticism and suggestions for other topics.

PATRICK KELLY
PO Box 103
Mount Freedom, NJ 07970

PFKJ@optonline.net